# THE BATTLE FOR T
## *The Church and Rud*

## By

## Ven. A. P. Shepherd DD. 1885—1968
*Archdeacon of Dudley, Canon of Worcester.*

An Anthology Compiled by and with an Introduction

By

David Clement.

# THE BATTLE FOR THE SPIRIT
*The Church and Rudolf Steiner*

**Copyright**
Photograph and all the Ven. A. P. Shepherd's writings
in this volume © Mary K. Barnsley
Introduction © David Clement 1994.

**ALL RIGHTS RESERVED.**
No part of this publication may be reproduced, stored in a
retrieval system, or transmitted, in any form or by any means,
electronic, mechanical, photocopying, recording, or otherwise,
without the prior permission of **Anastasi** ^Ltd.

**ISBN 0 9524403 0 X**

First Published 1994 By
**ANASTASI** ^Ltd.
Broome Nr. Stourbridge W. Mids. DY9 0HB

Printed and Bound in Great Britain by
**Biddles** ^Ltd.,
Guildford and King's Lynn.

Cover by Andy Oldacre

## DEDICATED TO

**Mildred Kirkcaldy** (née Robertson Nicoll)
who has taken the greatest interest and given much help in the
production of this book — and has had to wait several years to see it in
print — in her 97th-year.

To her Dr. Shepherd wrote on 12th March 1952:

*"I think my book ('The scientist of the Invisible') has benefited
enormously by the intervention of our book ('The Redemption of
Thinking' which they translated and edited together) and I feel I owe
very much to having worked with you, with your acute mind and
unfailing literary sense".*

i

# ACKNOWLEDGEMENTS.

To Mary Barnsley, the daughter of Dr. Shepherd, I am most grateful not only for putting at my disposal all her father's relevant papers, letters, articles etc.; but also for her interest and encouragement.

I would also like to thank all those who helped me with suggestions, advice and encouragement, in particular Owen Barfield, John Lees, Pearl Goodwin, Ralph Brocklebank and Sevak Gulbekian.

My thanks are also due to the Editor of the Birmingham Post for his kind permission to print some of the articles Dr. Shepherd wrote for that paper and the BBC for their permission to print his five minute talks in the "Lift up Your Hearts" Series in 1956.

# TABLE OF CONTENTS

# INTRODUCTION

To anyone who knew him, calling to mind Arthur Shepherd as he was—vital, warm, and human—is not difficult. A. C. Harwood, who was chairman of the Anthroposophical Society in Great Britain of which Shepherd became a leading member, used to refer to him as "the youngest member of my council." This was when Shepherd was in his eighties! He kept to the end his youthfulness of mind that showed itself in a zest for life and an enthusiasm for its possibilities that was infectious.

He was indeed a rare man; a faithful son of the church of England, who in his middle years was able to recognise the new revelation that Rudolf Steiner had brought; and he saw clearly what this could mean to all Christians; a new understanding; a new hope. Although he spoke tirelessly whenever he could, only a few individuals here and there were able to understand his vision. The most notable was the late Archbishop William Temple, who at the end of his life asked Shepherd to advise him on what of Steiner he should read.

It was in Barbados that Arthur Shepherd was born, in 1885. His father's family had a long association with Barbados and there still are Shepherds there to this day. He was the fourth child of eight, of whom the first died soon after birth. At the age of five he was brought to this country. His father, having qualified as a doctor at Edinburgh, began practising in Barbados; and only returned to this country on account of his wife's health. He then set up his practice in Cardiff. Arthur's mother[1] died when he was 14. It was she who told him, still a child, that he should go into the church.

One can so easily picture the boy he must have been: bright, intelligent, taking an eager interest in all that was going on around him. The headmaster of his school said, when Shepherd was leaving to go to the University, "We only managed to scratch his skin." He went to the University of Wales and obtained First Class Honours in Classics. From there with a scholarship, he went to Jesus College, Oxford. Studying Classics again he got a Second Class Honours in Greats, that is, in both Classics and Philosophy. He took an active part in university life and being good at games, played both hockey and tennis for his college.

---

[1]  Arthur's mother's maiden name was Woolley, she was the aunt of Leonard Woolley the archaeologist.

Later he also played tennis for Northamptonshire. He enjoyed watching games all his life.

Arthur Shepherd was ordained in 1911 and became Curate of All Saints, Northampton and, in a few years, Vicar of St. James. There is a recollection of him in those days by a local boy named Donald Perkins [2] in a letter written many years later—"He was Vicar of St. James when I was a boy. I lived in his Parish, although I was not a member of his Church. I remember him well—a young, handsome, vigorous priest. He impressed me and I felt, when he passed me in the street, that I wanted to shake hands with him. This was surely something for a boy to feel about a parson! I met him again in 1943 when he attended the Christian Community conference at Heathcot. It was the time when I had come to 'cross-roads' in my life and I was so grateful for his warm interest and willingness to help. I met him again at a conference at Forest Row and finally at Albrighton Hall [3] when he came to the Act of Consecration and received communion from me. He was a Christian, a human being."

From Northampton he went to Leicester to St. James the Greater. It was there in 1931 that he received his Doctorate in Divinity.

His thesis was then published under the title "Sin, Suffering and God." As Dr. Shepherd, he came to Dudley in Worcestershire in 1932; and in 1934 he was appointed archdeacon. That is how we first knew him: the Archdeacon in his gaiters; and very well he looked in them.

Ultimately he became Canon Emeritus of Worcester and vice Dean of the Cathedral. At his death in 1968 his ashes were buried in the garth of the cathedral cloisters. Only a few yards away there is a window, dedicated to his only son, David, together with the sons of the Dean and Archdeacon of Worcester, all three killed in action in the Second World War. The Bishop of Worcester, Mervyn Charles Edwards, in his funeral address, likened Arthur Shepherd to Great Heart in "The Pilgrim's Progress" saying, "He was always ready to help those of us who could only stumble where he walked so fearlessly;" and added that "In his case the head always spoke through the heart."

He was active in many spheres, not only ecclesiastical. The Staffordshire Iron and Steel Institute, the oldest of its kind in the world, invited Shepherd year after year to speak at their annual dinner. He had a

---

[2] The late Donald Perkins became a minister of the Congregational Church and later a priest of the Christian Community, Heathcot, near Aberdeen, which was, for a time, a centre of the Christian Community.

[3] Albrighton Hall, Shropshire, also at one time a centre of the Christian Community.

great sense of humour and a fund of good stories. I remember once returning with him and his family from Stratford and a Shakespeare play. We stopped at a pub and he started to tell stories, which he did very well and with considerable gusto! Being partially deaf he spoke rather loudly and, not noticing the quiet which soon descended over the room, was astonished at the roar of laughter that suddenly burst out.

One of his grandsons, Michael Shepherd, tells how as a young boy he used to stay with his grandfather in Worcester. They would often go for walks together and perhaps watch a cricket or football match. Then he would speak freely to his grandfather feeling understood and encouraged and never "talked down to!" Arthur Shepherd had a natural affinity to children of all ages. John Pearce-Higgins, the Vice Provost of Southwark Cathedral, after his death, wrote, "...Arthur Shepherd was one of the most loveable and human persons I have ever known. May I recall an anecdote. When staying with us at Putney, I awoke about 2a.m. to hear one of my small children calling. I got up and went down the passage, only to find that Arthur Shepherd, whose bedroom was opposite the child's, had anticipated me and I heard him call out 'alright, darling, I am coming!...'"

As an example of the help he gave to anyone in distress, here is a letter he wrote to a young couple who had just heard from their doctor that their child was a Mongol, or as it is now called, Down's Syndrome:

*"We have heard from Mary of the great shock that has come to you and Malcolm in the discovery that your baby son is a mongol child and we feel deeply for you in your sorrow and disappointment. Nothing I can say can take this from your hearts at the present time, but I am writing to suggest, if I may, some ways in which you may look at this."*

What follows next demands quotation in full, not only because it illustrates Shepherd's Christian wisdom but also because of its potential value to a reader who might be similarly afflicted.

*"The increase in the number of these children in the last century is very strange, and they are born to parents of all levels of culture and character, with no trace of heredity, nor the likelihood of repetition. Therefore, you will not ask "why should this happen to us?", because on earth there can be no clear answer to that question. Nevertheless, it helps one to remember that this child is not only 'your little son', but a spirit being, limited in the physical equipment with which he has to face his earth-experience, and that in this, he is*

3

*largely dependent upon you both to succour him in this task. Perhaps that is the answer to the question, "why did this happen to us?"*

*Again, though it is sad to think that he will never have the full mental equipment of the average human being he will suffer far less than a child born with some physical deformity, such as a club foot or a disfiguring birth mark, which he would have to carry all his life in full consciousness, which might deeply affect his character and his disposition. The mongol child is completely unconscious of his mental limitation, in place of which he has an abundant capacity for love and affection, which, in the right atmosphere gives him an entirely happy life. I have met many such children at Clent Grove whose happiness seems to bubble over. I have also seen some of the wonderful examples in which wise and loving training has produced a gentle, but quite satisfying, mental development.*

*If you ask me 'why should this happen to this child?', I should of course not be able to give you a complete answer, but believing, as I do, that none of us lives only one life on earth, I should feel that maybe out of his past experience, he needs an earth life where mental development is restricted that he may develop a soul-experience in love, and that, in this, he has chosen—or may be it was chosen for him—that you should be the parents who would sustain him with your strength and love.*

*Again, if you ask me 'why would such things be in the world at all?' I would say, that we know from the world around us and from our knowledge of our own hearts, how deeply evil and error have entered into God's plan, so deeply that Christ had Himself to carry the full burden of it, that in the end he might lift it from man's shoulders. Meanwhile, we are all caught up in the net of human suffering and sorrow, sometimes as sufferers, sometimes as saviours; and the measure of our strength in accepting that which has fallen upon us of this burden is the measure in which we perfect our own character by sharing in the redemptive suffering of Christ.*

*Out of this attitude of brave acceptance comes in the end strength and peace."*

In the Church Shepherd was active in Convocation and Church Assembly for many years; speaking frequently and often very much to the point. His daughter Mary tells how much it meant to him when he heard in Convocation someone speak of the threefold being of man—body, soul and spirit; the true composition of man which now-a-days is reduced to body and soul—or even only body.

4

He was a good administrator and a successful Treasurer of the Cathedral. On the occasion of his resigning the Archdeaconry of Dudley in 1951, William Cash the then Bishop wrote in the Worcester Diocesan Messenger "It is very difficult to express on paper what Dr. Shepherd has meant to me and to the Diocese. He has taken on an ever increasing burden in the multiplicity of his activities, and has won the affection and gratitude of everyone by his unselfish service. His committee work alone has taken up an immense amount of his time, for he threw himself, with unstinted generosity, into the whole life of the Diocese. His work on the Board of Finance was in many ways quite outstanding, and when Mr. Ottewell died and we were left without a Diocesan Secretary, it was Dr. Shepherd who came to the Board of Finance practically daily and helped in the office and guided its work with splendid success."

"But while this central work of the Diocese was outstanding, Dr. Shepherd was best known among the clergy by his constant visits to the parishes. He must have travelled many thousands of miles in his intimate touch with the clergy of his Archdeaconry. No parish was too small for his attention, and he was recognised as the personal friend of the clergy and their families. He knew intimately the hardships and difficulties of them all in these hard times. He was a great administrator and equally great friend."

In the midst of this very active life he published in 1941 "The Eternity of Time" to which Archbishop Temple wrote a foreword.

Shepherd was speaking about this book to a meeting of young men, when one of them said "but that is what Rudolf Steiner said", to which Shepherd replied "Who is Rudolf Steiner?" That is how he first heard of Rudolf Steiner.

As with all he undertook in his life, as soon as he realised the scope and importance of Anthroposophy (the name Rudolf Steiner gave to his teaching) he turned to it with his whole heart and mind. Many were the hours he spent in those days with Fried Geuter [4] at Sunfield Children's Home at Clent, in deep and earnest conversation. During the next few years besides meeting and speaking with many Anthroposophists (Dr. Walter Johannes Stein was one for whom he had a high regard and whom he tried to visit whenever he was in London) he read widely and, as was his wont, annotated the margins of each book and lecture-cycle. He started to write articles and lecture at Anthroposophical Conferences.

---

[4] Fried Geuter was the first Principal of Sunfield, Clent Grove, the first home in this country for children in need of special care based on Rudolf Steiner's teachings.

In 1953, together with Mildred Kirkcaldy, Shepherd edited Rudolf Steiner's three lectures on Thomas Aquinas, first translating them; but they both felt these lectures needed amplification before being put before the public. They therefore added an introduction, epilogue and appendices. Some three years later, when reviewing this book (which they named "The Redemption of Thinking"), A. C. Harwood wrote "It is a masterly example of how to make such a lecture course available to the public... available through being related to modern thought and modern issues." He goes on to say that not only did they make a "scholarly, terse and accurate translation but they have immensely enhanced the value of the text in three ways. Firstly they have annotated the lectures with valuable quotations from Steiner's own work in elucidation of many points and with extracts from contemporary writers which often serve to show how far he was ahead of his age. Secondly they have added appendices on a number of important matters—Dionysius (the Areopagite), Gondi-Shapur and Origen, to mention only three—that tell the reader just what he is likely to want to know. Thirdly, an Epilogue plainly aimed at readers who are making their first acquaintance with Steiner's work, gives a lucid description of the development of Steiner's thought and the nature of spiritual science. This last is an admirable addition; for a book of this calibre will surely find its way to many places where Anthroposophy has not yet penetrated."

But "The Redemption of Thinking" was not published straight away; the publishers first wanted a life of Steiner, as he was so little known. This was a disappointment but at the same time a challenge; and with characteristic energy Shepherd turned to his new task. In a little more than a year the book was written.

"A Scientist of the invisible—An Introduction to the Life and Work of Rudolf Steiner" came out in 1954 and "The Redemption of Thinking" in 1956. These two books have been a milestone on the Anthroposophical road out into the public. More than thirty years later they are both still in print.

In 1958 Shepherd published his last book, "Marriage was made for Man"; a forthright, compassionate work. "The value of Dr. Shepherd's book" wrote the Bishop of Worcester in his Introduction, "is its positive approach to the problem of marriage". It is beautifully written and is relevant to-day. He intended to write a further book on reincarnation. Though he gave it much thought in his last years, it was never written.

Shepherd had also written for a number of years, beginning in the early forties, many articles on religion for "The Birmingham Post." These articles were of high quality and dealt with the Christian path of pilgrimage—its ideal, its daily vicissitudes, its character-forming experiences—with the great festivals of the Christian year seen as the landmarks, and pointing the way to a gradually deepening understanding of what Shepherd liked to call "The Stairway of Being" and its gradual ascent.

A selection of these is included in the present book. The articles convey, in particular, his love and understanding of the Divine, which to-day is so little understood: the Divine Worlds; Christ as the Divine brother of man. These articles form the first part of this book. The second part is opened with a lecture Dr. Shepherd gave to members of the Anthroposophical Society under the title "The Battle for the Spirit" (later published in The Golden Blade) in which he researched the little known 8th Œcumenical Council of Constantinople of 869A.D. It was there that the idea of man as a being of body, soul and spirit, was reduced to one consisting of body and soul only. This is followed by a lecture in which Shepherd introduces Rudolf Steiner to his audience. After this follows the centre piece of this anthology: "Anthroposophy and the Christian Churches." It is here that Shepherd states without compromise the overwhelming importance of Steiner to modern Christianity: the revelations that enhance and enliven our beliefs and the path that every man can follow to experience these himself. Following the article on the Trinity in Man and Nature Part Two ends with Shepherd's account of the Incarnation as revealed by Steiner. This repays careful, thoughtful reading—without prejudice. It can then be a wonderful enhancement to the Gospel Stories. It is Shepherd's sane and human approach to Christianity which shines through all his writing that gives the spur to a serious consideration of all that Steiner taught. Part three brings to an end the main part of this anthology with five short statements on "Carrying Life's Burdens" that were originally broadcast by the B.B.C. in 1952 in the "Lift up your Heart" series. In the appendix is added one sermon, a fine example full of human warmth and Shepherd's fine historical sense. It was given on the occasion of the induction of Bishop Mort in Worcester Cathedral, in 1952.

It can perhaps be felt that there is a great difference between Parts One and Two. This is because Dr. Shepherd is addressing different people; the Birmingham Post articles were written for the public and Part

Two for those who already knew something of Steiner's teaching. They were all written over the same years. Part One could not, I feel sure, have been written with the same certainty and conviction if Shepherd had not already taken to heart Steiner's Christology.

In his obituary John Pearce-Higgins concludes "…It was this loveable humanity coupled with his profound wisdom and understanding that made him the really great man that he was, a greatness which the Church only in part recognised and rewarded, perhaps because of his off-beat views— views that I venture to think may well in time become close to the new orthodoxy of the future if the Church is to survive."

It is hoped that, taken together, the contents of this small book will convey something of the vision, the humanity and courage of this most loveable man.

*David Clement*

# PART ONE

# The Christian Year

"*The Holy Sprit is the power which will raise each man ever more and more above all that differentiates and separates him from others, and makes him a member of the whole of humanity on the earth; a power which works as a bond of soul between each and every soul, no matter in what bodies they may be.*"

RUDOLF STEINER — WHITSUN 1910.

# THE HOLY PRESENT

Time, Death, Judgement and Eternity are the four realities involved in the life of man, of which Advent reminds us, They are closely related one with the other,

Time is the earthly state of existence of man as spirit. Set in an eternal environment, which changes and evolves by laws over which it has no control, the human spirit finds its existence largely ordered by that environment, and it becomes conscious of itself by its awareness of that ever-changing relationship. But of all that can be so experienced, only that is at any time actually *experience*, which arises out of the immediate contact of the human spirit with its immediate environment. This we call the "present," All " past", experience can only be recovered as memory, a faint reflection of the experience itself.

What lies ahead, the "future", awaits the evolution of the environment which will largely determine it. It is almost entirely unpredictable and cannot be anticipated or accelerated.

Such is Time—*Death* is the inevitable step that each individual must take out of finite time-experience into an eternal existence. *Judgement* is the inevitable experience of a spirit that has passed through death and has become aware of its own being, fashioned out of the totality of its earthly experience, and finds that its eternal existence as spirit is dependent upon the qualities and creativity of that being and is bereft of any attachment to a controlled and inevitable environment. Such is *Eternity*.

* * *

Dread as the three final realities are, it is to the earthly time-experience that we must give all our heed, for out of it are being ever fashioned our eternal being and destiny. Think, then, with what wisdom and pity God set man in this condition of finite existence "making Time in making the World", as Plato put it. For man could only become conscious of himself by the experience of his relation to an ordered and evolving environment. Moreover, he could only get to know the true values of his developing spirit-being, because he could see them objectively in his past experience which he recovered in memory. Did the past return to him as actual experience, he could never view it objectively.

And how wonderful is that ever-moving "present" of man's conscious relationship to his environment! In it he lives in a real measure the life of a spirit-bring, for there his will makes contact with his environment with power to shape and order his own experience of it and with power even to shape and fashion the environment itself. In that ever-moving, holy moment of the "present", he is granted to share in the very creativity of God. Moreover, in that moment, lit by the perceived and applied values of his past experience—that is, by true repentance—he can even in a measure reshape the spirit pattern in himself, moulded by his now irrecoverable Past,

          *      *      *

But most of all—and only in that holy "present"—he can make contact in his spirit with the divine Christ, the ever-living One, Who stands for ever in every present moment, there and there only to be found of man, He it is and He only who, with man's consenting will, can completely change and refashion that result of man's past experiment and failure, until He makes it into the likeness of Himself,

The "present", then, is the significant and critical moment of our earthly existence, The past was ours but now eludes us; the future is not yet ours and will only be ours when it becomes the present, but the "now", the holy" present" is ours, ours to fashion with divine freedom, ours to share, if we will, with the Christ who came to heal and forgive and restore our spoilt past. The enemy of the "now" is sloth, that deep unwillingness to seize the holy and immediate present with the active will, that betrayal of the ever-present but ever-fleeting moment of man's divine creativity,

          *      *      *

" Life is full of the sound of closing doors." No wonder the saints have always regarded sloth as one of the chief causes of sin, and the deadly enemy of the human spirit. Advent recalls to us the ultimate realities of man's existence in order that it may inspire us to seize with both hands "the holy present". "The now is the acceptable time! ", it cries, "The, now is the day of salvation!"

## AWAKE TO THE LIGHT

"Awake out of sleep! The night is far spent, the day is at hand. Awake—to the light!" This is the Advent message. It is a strange reversal of accepted human symbols. To man, physical life is day and death is night; to St. Paul, earthly life is darkness and beyond death are the realms of eternal light. Or, to look at it in another way, we speak of the dark ages of the past and of our own as the age of enlightenment; yet from the point of view of the light of spirit reality we live to-day in an age of deepest darkness.

*     *     *

In his "Republic" Plato describes the life of man as of beings sitting in a cave with their backs to the entrance and only able to see thrown on the wall before them the shadows of objects borne along outside the cave. But, if we may strain the illustration, men have found that in the cave itself are endless objects of interest and also the means to light the, cave from within. Two generations ago the cave began to be flooded with electric light and the entrance to the cave was heavily curtained. If any light filtered through, it was lost in the artificial glare.

Now men knew far more about their cave, but they had come to think that there was no reality beyond it—only darkness. It was a comfortable well-lit world, full of endless possibilities, until in 1914 suddenly the fuses began to blow, and "the lights went out one by one in Europe". The darkness was impenetrable because it was so unexpected and though, after a few years, some of the lights were re-lit, one could no longer depend on the fuses.

*     *     *

Twenty-five years later there was an even more widespread blowing of the fuses, until suddenly the cave was rocked by so violent an explosion that men found that the same force which had lit their world could at any moment destroy it. Now they are beginning to wonder whether they can ever again rely on that power not to plunge them, not only into darkness, but into destruction.

It was a darkening age into which Christ came in this world. The cave was not so well-lit and the curtains were not so closely drawn, but already the outer light was fast becoming obscured. "I am the light of the world", Christ cried. "While you have the light, walk in the light, ere the darkness returns in which no man can safely walk." "In Him was light", wrote St. John, "and the light shone in the darkness, and the darkness comprehended it not".

They slew Him, as Plato had foreseen, and thrust him back through the curtains into what they, even then, thought was darkness. But in three days a divine hand swept the curtains back and for those who loved Him, the Light of the world was with them again and for a few weeks from time to time even the cave was lit by a heavenly radiance, And after the radiance passed from their actual sight, they still knew it in their hearts and souls as a light that should never fade, "seeing it is God that said

'Light shall shine out of darkness' who hath shined in our hearts, to give the light of the knowledge of the glory of God in the face of Jesus Christ".

&ast; &ast; &ast;

It is to prepare for the commemoration of the coming of that light at Christmas that Advent calls us and the message is "to awake out of sleep". For man to-day is in a deep sleep—or rather in a troubled dream—his senses dulled to reality, for all the vivid imagery of his dream. He will only awake when he realises that in his dream realities are reversed, that his day is night and that the night he fears is the light of eternal day. That light may even now flood the heart of each of us and guide our steps through the darkness, if into our heart is born once more the light of the world this Christmastide.

But more than that, shafts of that light are even now penetrating the bomb-rent curtains of our cave and, if we have eyes to see, the electric lights already begin to look tawdry. If we will only believe in that light, it will light up the wonders of our cave with even greater glories and reveal them in their true relation to the light-filled world around them. "Awake! Walk not as children of this darkness, but as the sons and daughters of light!"

## GOING, GOING—COMING!

The end of November is redolent of decay and death. The autumn colours have disappeared and every-where there is a murky greyness. The sky is covered with an unbroken pall of dull cloud, the leaves of summer lie in heaps of wet rottenness, except a few which still hang dejectedly from their branches. Over all there is the dank chilliness of heavy mist or the drip of ceaseless rain. With the coming of December there sounds a knell over the departed glory and beauty of the year. "Going, going—" but before the final word "Gone!" is spoken, suddenly the days begin to lengthen, frost dries up the ground and sends a tingling of life through our dulled veins, and over the corpse of summer is laid the unsullied mantle of snow, each crystal magnifying the beams of the wintry sun and bearing to the earth the resurrecting power of cosmic life-forces. Suddenly in some sheltered hollow the dark earth flickers with snowdrops, and the year's dirge of death changes to a note of expectation, "Going, going—Coming!"

&ast; &ast; &ast;

So, too, with the Church's year. Last Sunday we heard that last chapter of Ecclesiastes, haunting in the beauty of its metaphors and its cultured appreciation of the good things of life, all of which, however, must vanish completely at the onset of inevitable death. Nothing remains! "Then shall the dust return to the earth as it was and the spirit return to God who gave it. Vanity of vanities, all is vanity!"

To the Preacher life is just an endless series of repetitions, in which there is nothing new and nothing significant. All ends in the bathos of death. "Going, going—Gone!" Right through life there sounds this strain; even in youth it can be heard. "Going going, going—." The preacher of Ecclesiastes sounds the wistful pessimism of the ancient world at the end of the pre-Christian era.

❋ ❋ ❋

But to-morrow is Advent Sunday, with its rousing call, "Awake out of sleep! Get ready! Life's meaning is in the future, not in the past. Something is coming. It draws nearer to you every day. Awake to the dawning light of the new day!" The modern conception of history as moving to a goal first dawned on the Hebrew mind when Abraham was called to found a nation in whom all the other nations of the earth should be blessed. It was brought to fulfilment in Christianity. The pessimism of the ancient twilight of the gods was dispelled by the angelic message of good tidings of great joy: "Unto you is born a Saviour. Of His kingdom there shall be no end."

So the Advent message sounds each year. Awake! Hope! Keep faith with your hope. Open your hearts to the one who came and is ever coming, who proved that death is not the end, but just the swing of life's pendulum and leads by renewal to Himself as life's end. "I am he that liveth and was dead and behold, I am alive for evermore. I make all things new."

# THE MEANING OF JUDGEMENT

The certainty of judgement after death is present in some form in every religion. It was an essential part of the teaching of Christ. Men have pictured this judgement in the form of a court presided over by a Judge, whose sentence is complete acquittal or endless punishment. We must remember that men can only present spiritual truths in the form of pictures based on human experience. As long as we remember that they are only pictures, we can learn much from them, but taken literally they can be very misleading. Taken literally, this picture does not seem to fit

14

the character of God or the variability of guilt. So to-day it is widely rejected, and with it we reject the great truth that lies behind the picture.

What then is Judgement? There are two sayings of Christ about judgement in St. John's Gospel that seem to contradict one another. One is, "I came not to judge the world"; the other, "For judgement came I into the world." In the reconciling of these two statements we shall find the meaning of Judgement, namely, that it is the consequence of having the right or the wrong values, the things you think really matter in life, the standards by which you live.

It is plain from Christ's teaching that when we die we shall find ourselves in a state of being where there are different values to those on earth; things matter there that can be disregarded on earth, while things that mattered most on earth don't mean a thing.

It can be devastatingly painful to find yourself in a place where values are quite different from those you have always lived by. For in heaven you cannot get away from the true values. They force themselves upon you. Christ made this plain in the parable of Dives and Lazarus, in which, after death, the rich man, who had always lived in luxurious comfort, finds himself in torment, while he sees the man whom he had always regarded as utterly wretched, in perfect bliss. Abraham explains the situation to him in a few words. "On earth your values gave you a good time, but Lazarus's values did not give him a good time. Here Lazarus's values give him complete happiness, and yours give you—hell. But there is one thing more. You could at any time have put an end to Lazarus's misery, because it was not related to his values. But Lazarus cannot change yours here, for they are bound up with your wrong values. You can only end your suffering by changing your values, and that you must do yourself, and, as you are finding now, that is a very painful and difficult process."

Now we can begin to understand Christ's seemingly contradictory statements. "I did not come to sit in judgement on men's sins and pass sentence on them like a judge. But my coming has to do with judgement. I came to help men to get their values right." This He did all the time. Almost every time He spoke He was commending or condemning men's values. "Kindness matters more than correctness of behaviour," He said again and again to the respectable: "If you are blind and know it, I can help you to see, but if you are blind and think you can see everything I can do nothing for you." "It is not how much you give that matters but what it cost you to give it."

"Unchastity is wrong, but uncharitableness is worse." (So Professor Carstairs was right.) Why? Because it is easier to get the unchaste to see that their values are wrong than it is with the uncharitable. In fact, they are often most uncharitable towards the unchaste, caught in the consequence of their wrong values, and even when they are trying to get their values put right, as with Mary Magdalene and Simon the Pharisee. Then Christ weighed the values against one another.

Sometimes He changed men's values in a moment. Over a meal with Him the self-made Zacchaeus became convinced forever that a good conscience matters more than a good balance sheet. Christ also challenged the values of His own followers. "'Safety first' is no value for the Kingdom of Heaven," He said. "Only the willingness to risk everything for the right,"

There are two other sayings about judgement that are worth remembering. The one is by Christ. "If a man listens to Me and accepts My values, he will never have to face judgement." The other is by St. Paul "If you make a habit of judging yourself you won't need to be judged."

# THE CHRISTMAS MESSAGE

More and more widely throughout the world the Christmas season is recognised as the season of goodwill. Nor is this feeling merely one of jollity and good cheer: there is a deep longing everywhere for that "goodwill among men" that was the actual message of the first Christmas. There can be no doubt that in a real sense that message is reaching the soul of humanity, even where there is little or no understanding of the spiritual conditions on which it depends.

For Christians there is a far deeper significance in the Christian Festival, as the commemoration of that divine event, unique in human history, the birth of Jesus Christ, the intervention of God into the life of mankind at the level of physical sense-perceptible reality. "The word was made flesh and dwelt among us." Alas! there will be thousands of people, who will send Christmas cards with words and pictures of the beautiful Nativity stories, or will listen to the Nine Lessons Carol service, and yet miss the wondering joy which conviction of that event can bring. But, thank God, there will also be thousands whom the call "Come all ye faithful!" will bring, in the Midnight Mass or the early Christmas Communion, to the true commemoration of the Mystery, to the realisation of it as the pivotal event in all the earthly evolution of mankind, the interpretation of all that lay behind it, the potentiality of all that lay ahead of it.

* * *

Finally, there is to all those who recognise the spiritual message of Christmas another, more hidden, more personal significance. There is a deeper level of consciousness than that day by day physical consciousness in which Christmas is kept year by year in reverent, joyful commemoration. It is the level of our soul-life, that inner consciousness of which all of us, whether believing Christians or not, are aware. It is a realm independent of earthly time conditions, in which we walk the past as well as the present, in which our sins and failures are not cloaked by the surface picture of our earthly present.

* * *

In that realm the divine reality of Christmas is not merely a remembered past event, but an ever-present offer, that the child of our divine sonship may be born in that soul-realm, in the place where we habitually feed the ox of passion and the ass of self-will, that at his birth their desirous lowing and egotistic bray may be stilled. "As many as receive Him, to them gave He power to become the sons of God." The Christmas Festival is a special reminder in our time-consciousness of that ever-present divine offer—even if in the past we have refused it or, having accepted, have neglected it—that He in whose light we entered the world will ever rekindle that light by being born within us; the Everlasting Mercy unceasingly overshadowing the uncertain path of our soul-life.

> *For like a child sent with a fluttering light*
> *To feel his way along a gusty night*
> *Man walks the world. Again and yet again*
> *The lamp shall be by Fits of Passion slain;*
> *But shall not He who sent him from the door*
> *Relight the Lamp once more, and yet once*
> *more?*

# FESTIVAL OF DIVINE BIRTH

It is often brought forward as an argument against the Christian significance of the Christmas Festival that it coincides with the age-long festivals of the winter solstice and the return of the sun, which have existed from the most ancient times in all religions. Such an argument is based upon an entire misunderstanding of the situation. The founders of the great religions of the ancient world felt man to be an integral part of Nature, and in her rhythms and ordered changes they saw the actual working of a divine plan, relevant to man. Man, faced with the struggle for existence, especially in countries of long winters, felt joy in the knowledge that the darkest days were past and that the light was returning; but he was also led to see that that was the expression of the light of the spirit, reborn and rising again and again in the darkness of human nature. It was later, when man had lost spirit vision, that he took the natural objects themselves and their processes and made them his gods. It was against this that Hebraism and, later, Christianity bore witness, and taught man to look again, behind Nature to Spirit.

But the position to-day is quite different. We are not in touch with Nature, she has become a stranger to us. The Earth is not our mother, but only the material field of our environment, to use or misuse as we will, for our profit or pleasure. Even religious leaders shut their eyes to the obvious relation of the great Christian Festivals to the recurring crises of the natural year, the spring and autumn equinoxes, midsummer and midwinter.

But our ancient forefathers did not see these relationships only as accidental or illustrative. They saw them as an annual setting forth of a spirit reality, which would itself one day be manifest in actual human history. They were taught by the teachers of the Mysteries to see in the returning power of the sun, which would certainly result in the bursting forth of light and growth in the spring, proof that one day there would return to man the warmth of the spiritual sun, which would bring light and order to the spiritual darkness and chaos of human feeling and will. The degenerate orgies of the Roman Saturnalia bore as little resemblance to the ancient winter festival of the Rebirth of Light, as a great deal of the commercialised and sentimentalised Christmas festivities of the present day bear to the Mystery of the Divine Incarnation. It was no adjustment to these popular festivities, but a realisation that the Christian Christmas was the historical fulfilment of man's ancient longings, that led the Christian Church of the fourth century to attach to the Winter Solstice Festival the birthday of Jesus, which formerly had been variably observed.

We are inevitably—and not unwillingly—caught up today into the social, festive side of Christmas, which is for many others devoid of all religious significance. Let us not lose its deep significance for ourselves. Let us create in our hearts an Imagination, that is, an idea so inwardly dwelt upon that it becomes a reality, not only to our mind, but also to our heart and will. Let us realise that Christmas, the ever-recurring festival of the birth of the divine Child in the darkness of a violent and unbelieving world, is the guarantee that the divine light can ever be reborn in the darkness of our own sinful nature; that God taking human form is the guarantee that our bodies can be temples of the Spirit: and that Emmanuel, "God with us," will become Easter, "God for us," and Whitsun, "Christ in us, the hope of glory."

# THE TURNING-POINT OF HISTORY

The beginning of a New Year makes us for a moment conscious of the passing of history, but for most people the picture that arises is that of life's events being carried away on the flow of time rather than of time as the significant setting of human life. There was never an age when the study of history was more intense and scientific than it is to-day: there was never an age when the study of history was more meaningless.

The Jewish people were almost the earliest race to have a historical sense in the modern use of that phrase and to them history always had the fullest meaning. For they traced its beginning back to the act of God in creation and they felt more and more that it was leading to a divinely-ordained end in which their destiny as a people would be consummated.

*     *     *

This sense of a divine origin of history was not, as is so often stated, a fantasy of primitive imagination, but the direct perception of a primitive clairvoyance common to all humanity. Gradually this conviction ceased to be a matter of vision but it was still accepted unquestioningly. In the same way the awakening sense of a divinely-ordained end arose out of clairvoyant apocalyptic vision.

The Christian Faith took over and kept this Jewish interpretation of history and all through the middle ages of Europe man, with far less science of history than today, saw far more meaning in it as proceeding from God to God. Though with him it was no longer vision, but faith in a divine revelation, it gave him a sense of human significance and of the eternal worth of the individual that is largely missing to-day.

With the modern scientific idea of the world as having its origin in some stellar occurrence and its end in a general conflagration or a gradual

19

cooling of the earth, and of man as evolving at a certain stage in that earth-process, history can no longer have any meaning for man. It is only an incident. This historical scepticism has infected the thought even of many who profess the Christian faith.

* * *

But to the Christian the meaning of history hinges on more than faith in its divine origin and end. It hinges on an event at its *centre* , the divine event of the Incarnation. That is why Christmas stands so appropriately on the threshold of the New Year, because the Incarnation is the clue to the meaning of history. It is as though, with the dimming of man's vision of his divine origin and end, God brought divinity into the midst of human history, clothing it in physically visible terms of time and space, through which the eye of faith might discern the divine glory. To such an eye the Incarnation becomes the turning-point of history, whose meaning is revealed, not in its end or origin, but in its relation to that centre point. In the Incarnation is the arresting of the descent of human history and the beginning of its long and arduous ascent, and a clear-eyed view perceives that fact in spite of the many moral and spiritual disappointments of our day. For it is only but yesterday that many parts of the human race have come into conscious contact with that "fulcrum" of the Incarnation—and ascent is inevitably slow. But the man who, in his own life, has found the Incarnation a turning-point from dissent to slow ascent has a certainty of the meaning of history, as hinging on this same divine event, that no sceptical scientific materialism can dispel. To each one of us the Christmas festival offers every year this experience and this certainty.

## EPIPHANY:—THE THREE WISE MEN

To-morrow is the feast of the Epiphany or the Manifestation of Christ to the world. The first implication of that is something very vital to Christianity, namely that it is not the discovery of God by man, but a self-revealing of God to man. The story specially connected with to-morrow is the Visit of the Three Wise Men, directed to Bethlehem by the heavenly light that had announced to them Christ's coming. But there are other incidents of God's self-revelation—to the Blessed Virgin Mary, to the Shepherds at Bethlehem and to Simeon and Anna in the Temple. It is of the essence of the Christian gospel that it is good news from God, His plan, His message, His achievement—a deed of God in time and space. The nineteenth century humanism that tried to interpret Christianity as man's highest approach to and clearest revelation of the Divine is not the gospel of the New Testament. It lacks the tremendous significance of divine initiative.

*　　*　　*

On the other hand this self-revelation of God did not *compel* man's recognition, it was no "sign from heaven" that men could not deny or refuse. There were only a very few who recognised and responded to it, lovers of divine wisdom, men of simple heart or of pious expectation. They were drawn to it by faith and that faith penetrated through the veil of apparently ordinary humanity at which other men's vision stopped. Nor was the faith that led them merely an intellectual proposition which they were induced to accept. The message of the angels, the appearance of the star, spoke to their deepest feelings, arousing a sense of expectation which they could not have defended logically, but which they were prepared to follow. "We saw the star and have come." "Let us go to Bethlehem and see." "We have waited for the consolation of Israel and mine eyes have seen." It is always so in spiritual revelation. It is always given to men's deepest *feelings* and, in trusting them and acting upon them, the revelation becomes a certainty.

*　　*　　*

It makes all the difference to the value and potency of Christianity in our daily life, especially in these difficult times, whether or not we see it as an Epiphany, a self-revelation of God to man in the great divine deed of Christ. It frees it from every limitation of time and place, it lifts it out of the past into the present. That historical event in the reigns of the Roman Emperors Augustus and Tiberius becomes the eternal attitude of God to man, the deed that takes upon it all human sin from Adam to the Day of Judgement, that is wrought now, to-day, on our altars, in our hearts, out of the grace and ever-flowing love of God to meet our modern needs and problems.

But remember, it can still only be apprehended by faith, and that, not just an acceptance of orthodox dogma, but an awakening of response in the deepest feelings of our heart to the gospel of that divine Epiphany and a patient obedience of our will to those feelings, issuing at last in a certainty of conviction. Was not the final testimony of St. Paul's life given in the words, "I was not disobedient to the heavenly vision."?

# BORN FROM ABOVE

The account in the third chapter of St. John's Gospel of the interview between Christ and Nicodemus is a mysterious passage, whose spiritual revelations and intimations can be apprehended only in deep meditation. The author of the Gospel is twice at pains to establish the historical identity of Nicodemus, and so disposes of the idea that this passage is a mystical imagination. Nicodemus was a Jewish initiate, "a master in Israel." Jesus called him. But he recognised in Jesus a greater initiate— "a teacher sent from God"—and he sought His deeper knowledge.

Jesus's answer startled him, "Except a man be born from above, he cannot behold the Kingdom of God," the spirit world. "How can a man be born a second time?" Nicodemus asks, "I am not speaking," replied Jesus, "of a physical birth, but of a spiritual birth." The Jewish initiates, like all the initiates of the ancient world, sought to raise themselves to a knowledge of the spirit world by a transformation of their physical powers. Baptism, which John the Baptist practised, was one of the last means of such transformation. But John said, "It will pass. One is coming who will baptise, not with water, but with the spirit." "No man," said Jesus, "can ascend to heaven except first his higher self descend from his spiritual home and be born into earthly life."

So it was that when He, who was both Son of God and Son of Man— the divine image and creator of man's being (Col. III.10)—would lead man to heaven, He had Himself to descend from heaven and be born into an earthly human life, and thence ascend to heaven again. Those who recognised and received Him in that earthly life, to them gave He the power themselves to grow on earth into sons of God, whose origin was not in the physical world and the human nature in which they lived, but in the divine world of their Heavenly Father.

Christ speaks the same word to us as to Nicodemus. "You can attain to heaven only by being born from above into human earthly life. That higher self of yours, which is itself spirit, can attain its true fulfilment only by realising itself in earthly form." How can we achieve it? The earthly pull is too strong for us. We can achieve it only by uniting our own higher self with Him who for our sakes trod the path of earthly incarnation.

This does not mean shaping ourselves to some particular ecclesiastical or conventional picture of Christ, nor even applying rigidly to our lives today the pattern of the earthly life He chose to lead for us nineteen centuries ago. It means realising that we are spirit beings with a divine nature, who can come to our spiritual fulfilment—"ascend to our glory"—only by first descending into earthly life and then, in that earthly pilgrimage, uniting our higher, inner self with Him, the Alpha and Omega of our being, who for us and for our salvation trod the path of human fulfilment, from heaven to earth and through the earth to heaven.

# DIVINE IMAGINATION

Most of our experience of the world and our fellow men presents itself to us in the form of pictures, and when we look back in memory its whole content is a succession of pictures. But the most wonderful power of imagination or image-forming, and that which sets man high above the animal world, is the power of fashioning pictures of that which we have not actually seen, of clothing our ideas with picture-form, and of expressing these picture-forms in painting or sculpture, in music or poem.

Now in religion we are dealing with subject matter that is for the most part beyond physical experience—God and the world of spirit—and though Christianity is based on an historical life, the events of that life are outside our personal experience and are conveyed to us only by written narratives. By faith we accept these as true, and also give consent to the theological conclusions and teaching based upon them. That is an appeal to our thinking and our will, but unless it is also accepted by our feeling, it will never exercise a real compulsion upon us, and in life's crises it may easily desert us. Thus there is in religion an especial need for Divine imagination, the forming of what we believe into pictures, on which our heart may dwell and in which our beliefs come to life.

Especially in worship and in prayer do we need to exercise our imagination, for without it worship can easily become formal and lacking in reality. A great deal of the criticism that is directed against public worship arises from the fact that the critic has failed to exercise upon it, as a worshipper, his own imagination.

It is characteristic of English worship that the worshipper always wishes to take vocal part in it and feels that, if he does not do so, his worship is unreal. Yet it is silent participating listening that imagination can best work. Most of my worship takes place in a cathedral and one of the objects of a cathedral is to render worship in the most beautiful music and singing, for which there is a trained and constantly practised choir. Yet there are some visitors who think they can take no part in the worship unless they sing themselves, and not infrequently they intrude upon the offering of beautiful music with their untrained voices, though they would not think of intruding upon the music of an oratorio.

Of course mere listening, even critical musical listening, is not worship. But it is my experience that listening with imagination, forming the words and music into a picture of worship ascending to God, gives the deepest awareness of its spiritual meaning and a sense of sharing *with one's soul* in the act of worship. Familiar parts of Church worship, the *Te Deum*, the Magnificat and the Psalms, are lifted to a new level of spiritual reality by this practise of divine imagination.

As I have said, it is only out of individual, listening silence that spiritual imagination is born. In fact, our hymns, that part of our public worship in which there is a recognised right of congregational participation, seldom achieve the full possibilities of their spiritual message, because we never make use of them in listening stillness. It is a revealing experience to make a well-known hymn the silent, imagination-filled content of our private prayer. Imagination is only part of worship, but the absence of it robs worship of intensity, and faith of an ever-quickened certainty.

# AND WAS MADE MAN

The central doctrine of the Christian Church, the Incarnation of God in Man, was from the first a mystery over which there were the fiercest theological disputes. The Church herself held firm to the doctrine without officially explaining it, but in thought and worship tended to emphasise the divine aspect of the Christ.

It was not until the nineteenth century, with the growth of scientific materialism and of the comparative study of history and religion, that a reaction set in, and Christian thinkers tended more and more to emphasise the human nature of Christ; as the carpenter of Nazareth, a Jew with the limitations of outlook of his time and race.

＊　　　＊　　　＊

Everything divine or super-human was whittled away from the Gospel narrative, and with the growth of interest in "the Common Man," emphasis was laid upon the supposed lowly birth of Christ—"a common man of common earth"—though, in point of fact, He was "of the royal house and lineage of David." Moreover, there developed a tendency to feel that it was essential that the Saviour should have been a man "just like one of us."

All this tended to depreciate the authority of Christ's teachings and sayings, and to reduce Him merely to the level of an average Jew of the first century. Now all this is based on the false assumption of equality between men, with "the common man" the yardstick of all.

This is the reverse of the truth. In every generation there are men who stand head and shoulders above their fellows; Moses, Buddha, Socrates, Leonardo da Vinci, Shakespeare, Bacon, Einstein, Schweitzer. In many instances they completely transcend the vision and concepts of their own age. They are the saviours and pioneers of the race.

The fact that they share the physical characteristics of human nature does not bind them to the level of "the common man." This historical fact dispels any idea of the equality of men, or that the saviour of a race is to be looked for in " a man just like ourselves."

If this is true of men, how infinitely more true is it of One whom we believe to be the incarnation of the divine. In this belief, the divine is not brought down to the lowest common measure of humanity, but humanity is raised to its highest level, "to the full stature of a man as it is in Christ Jesus." If there have been men whose wisdom and spiritual insight soared far above the average level of their age and race, with how much more certainty and independence of environment would the divine wisdom of Christ express itself in His human words and deeds.

*     *     *

The humanistic viewpoint is not so strong to-day in theology, yet in face of the great discoveries of our scientific age, there are very many Christians who feel that the utterances of a man two millennia ago cannot dispute the pronouncements of science to-day.

The best evidence of the superlative eminence of Christ is given by the men of His own day. Those who knew of Him only in His human background said of Him "Never man spake as this man." But those who had an intimation of His divine origin spoke with an even deeper certainty of perception. "We beheld His glory, glory as of the only-begotten of the Father, full of grace and truth."

# THE GOSPEL STORY

From Epiphany we follow, in the Sunday Gospels and Lessons, the earthly ministry of Christ. His teaching and His works of healing, until at

Holy Week we arrive at the central fact of the Christian Gospel, the drama of His Passion, Death and Resurrection. It is "the Gospel Story," which for eighteen hundred years was accepted unquestionably by Christians just as it is recorded by the Evangelists.

The last century of universal criticism produced a different attitude, both to the story itself, and to the records of it. Beginning with Renan, through Schweitzer's and Glover's "Jesus of History," the story was almost whittled down to its merely human elements, out of whose perfection alone any divinity was derived. The records too were denied almost any historical trustworthiness.

* * *

In the early part of this century there was a tendency to dramatize the story in a spirit of sentimental humanitarianism. There were also scholarly renderings of the story into modern English, in the somewhat pathetic expectation that easy comprehensibility would evoke belief. Twenty-five years ago English theologians awoke to the realisation that the Gospel records are inherently and intrinsically concerned with the supernatural, and the latest modern translation by E.V. Rieu, in the Penguin Classics, seeks to convey that impression, in a more faithful rendering of its implication in the Greek original.

But a new understanding of the essential supernatural content of the Gospel story has lately arisen, an understanding of the reality of the consciousness of the supersensible in the men of that day, and of the originality of its working in the story, in which the divine is not merely the flower of the human, but is the creative "Word of God" manifesting itself under human forms. In his book "The New Man", Dr. Maurice Nicoll revealed this essential element in Christ's teaching, showing that it carried a meaning that could not be discerned in the mere literalness of the parable, still less in its colloquial rendering in another tongue. Hard to follow at times, Dr. Nicoll reveals the reality of a spirit-mystery awaiting those who can penetrate into and behind the parabolic form.

Recently there has been published a yet more complete exposition of the essential spiritual origin and content of the story and the records, in "The Three Years", translated from the German of Emil Bock. Here we study the records against a background in which spirit is a recognised reality no less than matter, in which spirit experience is so actual that it is described in the same terms as physical happenings. It is a background that will be more and more confirmed by a study of the Dead Sea Scrolls and the Egyptian Codices. And as with the story, so with the records. They are seen to be based upon the spiritually developed capacity to relive past experience, rather than the mental ability to recollect and record objective facts. In this their variants are seen to be evidence of their genuineness.

*   *   *

It is an interpretation of the Gospel Story in which we never lose awareness of the divine origin and initiative in human redemption. The key to the understanding of the Mystery is not the rudimentary scientific outlook of first century humanity, but the continual self-manifestation of the Christ, in His achievement of the supreme event in human evolution. In the Synoptic Gospels it is represented in its impact, varying yet unquestionably identical, upon three types of human response. In St. John it breaks through the human barrier, until, as Dr. Rieu puts it, "we feel that we are hearing Jesus speak through John."

"The Three Years" is a difficult book; it will provoke thought, and criticism. But it throws open the door to a new level of understanding of the spiritual significance and content of the Gospel Story.

# FREEDOM OR SERVITUDE

There is no instinct more universal in the British people than that each individual should be able freely and effectively to exercise his will and express himself. But this ideal is far from being attained. There is no greater need for mankind to-day than the freeing of the human will. We live in an age of action in all directions, action on the grand scale, effected for the most part by powerful machinery and controlled by huge organisations, multiple firms, trade unions, political parties, State departments. We cannot stand outside them and so we submit ourselves to them and even identify ourselves with them. We obey their rules, we think their thoughts, we utter their shibboleths—but we are not really ourselves. We may even lose the power to be ourselves.

*   *   *

The same danger confronts us all in our private life. We are so beset with the material world in which we live, its objects become so necessary or so desirable to us, that we tend to regard our relation to them as primary and as constituting our very self. So it is with our feelings, our passions, our likes and dislikes; we accept them, we hardly ever question them and at last we identify ourselves with them. When we say "I," we think of our self as consisting of such and such surroundings and possessions, such and such passions and prejudices. And yet those things are not the real "I," the real self. We should be able to see our self quite

27

apart from our material setting, to detach our self from the emotions and desires which assail us. But these things have captured us, they have branded the mark of their ownership upon our very faces, they have made us the expression of themselves.

*   *   *

It was from this servitude that Christ came to set us free and it is to obtain that liberty that we are called to train our wills. That is why each year the Church calls us to a special season of self-discipline and self-training, in which we deliberately break free of the bond of some material habit our pleasure and for a while renounce it, in which we concentrate more on the spiritual, the real nature of our true self. In the Church of England this self-discipline is not rigidly imposed, though each of us is called to observe it, and this Anglican belief in spiritual freedom throws a greater measure of responsibility on the individual. His own individual will must enter into his struggle. The challenge is a hard one, but if we rise to it, we shall be on our way to achieving that freedom to which Christ calls us and without which we can never be men.

# PRACTICAL CHRISTIANITY

Last Sunday on the very threshold of Lent, the Church in the epistle for the day, presented us with that tremendous warning of St. Paul, that all for which Lent stands is worthless if we have not love. All spiritual attainment, all self-discipline, even to the point of utter mortification, all generosity of giving, all these—apart from love—are worth nothing. We know the passage well, not only for the beauty of its language, but because it at once strikes a responsive chord in our modern hearts. For we mostly dislike self-discipline and asceticism and say that all that matters is that we should love one another—by which we generally mean that we should have warm, friendly feelings of fellowship and goodwill towards one another. Of course the warning was very necessary in St. Paul's day, when everyone expected religion to be a matter of rule and observance, and when love between men was a very "new commandment," not accepted by mankind. But at first sight it doesn't sound so timely to-day, when to most people religion is a matter of opinion and discussion or of feeling and preference—and not something which must be expressed in terms of the will, in deed and life.

We hear all sorts of opinions expressed to-day as to why people do not come to church and all sorts of remedies are offered. One of the chief reasons is that people have come to regard Christianity as something which people like as other people like music or some form of art, and which they follow when they feel like it. They do not conceive of it as something of vital concern to man's practical life, a matter of intrinsic worth or objective reality. That too, is why most people are so little affected by the fact that their neighbours are professing Christians. No one is much concerned about his neighbour's hobbies or emotional preferences, but only that which makes for a different way of living. Of course we have no excuse for this point of view, for Jesus made it plain that Christianity is "doing," or it is nothing. "However interested you are," He said, "in what I say, however much it thrills you, if you do not put it into practice, you are bound to crash. Besides you will never understand it; because it is only when you make a determined effort to put it into practice that you really begin to grasp the truth of it." That is why so many people to-day are "all at sea" about their faith. Lent calls us to express our faith in terms of will and action.

So perhaps we begin to wonder whether the Church was wise to choose this passage, with its apparent discounting of asceticism, unless it be accompanied by love. Then we read the passage again and find that we made a fundamental mistake at the beginning. For the love of which St. Paul speaks has little to do with feeling , but everything to do with will and action. The modern world has desecrated love by conceiving of it almost entirely in terms of feeling, but St. Paul never thought of love in that way.

"Love shows kindness, however much it has been ill-treated, love never boasts nor seeks advantage, love takes no offence and forgives injuries "—and so on. What a picture of love in action! It would have been easier if Paul had left us with our spiritual accomplishments and our self-martyrdom. But we need these, too; for if they are worthless without love, love like this is impossible without them. "Now abideth Faith, Hope, Love—these three." Faith is the consecration of our Thinking, Hope the consecration of our Feeling, and Love the consecration of our Willing. "And the greatest of these is Love"—for alone of these three it has in it the actual experience of the eternal..

## KNOW THYSELF

"Know thyself." These two words were set over the portal to the ancient Mystery temples, as the key to the gateway to higher knowledge.

To-day man, in our Western civilisation, is more ego-conscious than he has ever been before, more self-assertive, more interested in self-study and self-analysis, more convinced that he can set the origin and destiny of man within the compass of materialistic scientific definitions. But man is never more likely to be self-deceived than when he is sure that he knows. In times of crisis he becomes doubtful as to whether his scientific certainties hold good, as the new philosophy of Existentialism indicates.

The Christian Church has always urged upon man a true knowledge of himself and in the season of Lent, with its three rules of fasting, almsgiving and prayer, we have a path to self-knowledge. Let us consider it. The more we understand and are able to control our material environment, the more prone we are to identify ourself with our relation to it, to regard our wealth and circumstance, our comfort and pleasure, as essential to our being. Here the first Lenten rule of fasting or self-denial has its significance. It is a deliberate cutting away from ourselves of one or more of the material things that we usually regard as essential or very desirable. It is a reminder and a discovery that the self lies deep beneath these material relationships and is not affected in its true being by their presence or absence, but only by its loyalty to its own ideals.

But asceticism is not enough by itself, for it can thrust the self into a condition of pride and isolation from its fellows, as in the case of the Stoic or the Pharisee. Still less than in material well-being is the true self to be found in spiritual isolation; for while the self is fundamentally independent of its material relationships, it is utterly dependent upon its relationships with other spiritual beings, its fellow men and women. So the second rule of lent is "almsgiving," the deliberate identification of our self with the needs and circumstances of others, and that not only in physical, but in mental and spiritual relationships. It is a great discovery of the nature of one's own self. "I first discovered what life meant," a working man once told me, "when I began to make a habit of doing what I could for others."

This is a great step in self-knowledge, but it only takes us part of the way. For the discovery that the soul lives in human relationships itself suggests that it must be possible to have relationship with the eternal source of all being and of all human relationships, with God Himself. Thus we have the third Lenten rule of "prayer," the entering of the self into conscious relationship with God, in which it will find its true being most fully realised. "This is eternal life," said Christ, "that men should know God." The prophet Micah presents this threefold path to self-realisation in words of sublime simplicity; "To do justly, to love mercy and to walk humbly with thy God."

# SELF-SATISFACTION

"Two men went up into the Temple to pray, the one a Pharisee, the other a Publican." We all know this parable, or if we have forgotten it we can read it for ourselves in the eighteenth chapter of St. Luke's Gospel. It is a parable that wins everyone's approval; its application seems so obvious—a self-satisfied hypocrite sneering at an honest penitent. We rather enjoy it, partly because we do not feel ourselves to be such hypocrites, nor do we feel that we stand in need of such abject penitence. Besides, it looks like a condemnation of the church-goer in comparison with the casual worshipper—and most of us are casuals.

*　　*　　*

But the parables of Jesus are not quite so obvious; they go much deeper. If they do not flash the searchlight of conscience into your own heart, you can be fairly sure you have missed their point. You have become one of those of whom Jesus said, "Hearing they hear and do not understand; and seeing they see but do not perceive".

The point of the parable is not the comparison of smug hypocrisy with honest penitence—certainly not to compare unfavourably the good-living, respectable man with the careless man-of-the-world. The Evangelist tells us just what Jesus means. He says: "Jesus spake this parable unto certain who trusted in themselves that they were righteous and despised others."

*　　*　　*

Indeed, to-day Jesus would probably have put the parable in another way. He might have said something like this: "Two men were walking down the street one Sunday morning, Robinson a sturdy successful-looking business man on his way to a day's golf in the country, and Smith, timid and conventional-looking, on his way to church. Said Robinson: 'Thank God I am an honest man, who accepts fearlessly the conclusions of modern science, and doesn't cling to outworn comfortable faiths or escapist beliefs. I do not pretend to be better than I am, and I accept the limitations of my human instincts. I do not go whining and puling to God about my faults or expect him to do for me what I ought to do for myself—like Smith there who goes to Communion every Sunday, though he cannot defend his beliefs in an argument, and his faults are apparent to anybody.' And Smith kneeling at the altar rail, conscious of his nervous irritability and his many inconsistencies, and wondering why he had not got the robust self-confidence of Robinson, murmured: 'I do not presume to come to this Thy Table, O merciful Lord, trusting in my own righteousness, but in Thy manifold and great mercies.' He went home a better man, but Robinson returned only a little more deeply sunk in his pseudo-scientific, egotistic self-complacency."

\* \* \*

No, the parable was not a question of hypocrisy. The Pharisee spoke the truth: he *was* a better-living man than the Publican, but he was self-complacent about it, and kept measuring his life by his own good points, and by the obvious defects of other men. How often had Jesus seen this deadening self-complacency on the faces of the Scribes and Pharisees, just as he had seen the Publican's experience in the face of Simon Peter, of Mary Magdalene and of Zacchaeus. What the parable says is this: "If you measure yourself by other men, you may be flattered, but you will deteriorate; if you measure yourself by God you will be humbled, but you will improve."

Moreover, it is this spirit of self-complacency and criticism that keeps men from understanding one another and, in the end, drives them in to irreconcilable opposition. If one man approaches another in this spirit, he can never really know him, because he holds before his eyes the screen of his own self-satisfaction. We English are a bit prone to do this. We are very proud of our natural English virtues—honesty and courage and independence of spirit—and we think they are indispensable qualities. If other men have not got these qualities we write them off as poor, inferior types, and yet all the while these other men often have good qualities which we do not possess. This is the real danger in the international situation to-day: the deepening rift between East and West is due to each side condemning the other in the light of its own standards; and so they never understand each other, and the rift between them widens.

\* \* \*

Meanwhile, let us turn the searchlight of this parable on our own heart; it is there that we must feel the challenge to our self-satisfaction. If we keep standing on the little mounds of the virtues which we fancy we possess, virtues which we fondly attribute to our own achievement, we shall get no higher. If we would attain to the real heights of virtue, we must first descend to the level plain of humility. We shall soon find that this descent becomes a path of ascent to the Hill of God, and a way of understanding and access to the hearts of our fellow men.

# THE DIVINE SACRIFICE

"No one taketh My life away from Me," said Jesus: "I lay it down of Myself." As we consider the story of Christ's betrayal and trial and crucifixion, our minds are overwhelmed with the cruelty and ingratitude and wickedness that could work this deed. This is particularly the reaction of our present age and especially of the young, who are always sensitive to injustice. There is a tendency however, in this reaction only to see the Cross in this light, with a sense of indignation and compassion, and to lose the awe and wonder of the Divine sacrifice, of God freely laying down His life for mankind.

How can we reconcile these two aspects of the Cross? There are some modern thinkers who declare that if the sacrifice of Christ was eternally decreed and was the deliberate act of Christ, then moral blame cannot attach to the human agents in that event. But the sin-hardened treachery of Judas, the unscrupulous malevolence of Caiaphas, the weak-principled vacillation of Pontius Pilate and the cruel blood lust of the mob are without question the responsible human factors in that fell deed.

\* \* \*

In what way, then, was it the act of Christ Himself? In that, when their will was set on His destruction, He did nothing to stop them. That He could have done this He Himself declared in the words that checked St. Peter's impulsive violence; "Thinkest thou that I could not pray My Father and He would immediately send Me more than twelve legions of angels?" But it was not only by supernatural means that Jesus could have defeated His attackers. Like a tragic refrain in the account of His trial the words recur, "He answered nothing." "He answered to them never a word." The only one to whom he replied was Pilate, for he knew that, humanly speaking, he was a pawn in a game which he did not understand. How often had Christ's answers in their sheer simplicity and moral greatness silenced His critics and tempters! How easily could He have confounded the false witnesses, or riddled before Pilate the high priest's accusations or carried away Herod into a royal intervention. He did none of these things. When He saw that men's wickedness was determined to compass His death, He did nothing to stop it.

\* \* \*

"He answered nothing." Is not that an exact picture of how God reacts to our sin and rebellion against Him? He does nothing, He says nothing, to prevent our deliberate wrongdoing and self-willed rebelliousness. It is the eternal sacrifice of God to man's moral freedom,

33

the price He deliberately pays that we may at length attain the divine nature in the willed freedom of sons and daughters of God. Thus it is that St. Paul speaks of Christ's death upon the Cross as "making plain God's righteousness in the passing over of the sins done aforetime, in the forbearance of God."

But the apparent triumph of wickedness is never final. The righteousness that seems stricken down rises again, to comfort the faithful and to challenge and plead still with the world to win its heritage of moral freedom. Those who, like St. Paul, come to know that He, whom they themselves crucified, lives and reigns, find in the risen Righteousness the birth in them of a new life. When that happens to you or me then our Easter has dawned.

# THE EASTER VICTORY

To many Christians, the victory of Easter is merely the victory of life over death; the assurance that death is not the end; the hope of immortality. Our Saviour, crucified by wicked men, rose from the dead. Therefore we, forgiven by the death which He endured for us, shall ourselves pass after death to life eternal. This however, is for us no victory, but only a deliverance. Yet Christ promised us a victory, and St. Paul and St. John both speak of it.

The Easter victory goes far deeper than this. It is the victory of spirit over flesh, over the material world, not only in surviving it, but here and now, in the earthly life itself. It is the certainty that man himself is spirit, and as such, can triumph over all that flesh or the world can bring upon him.

\* \* \*

More and more, in the centuries that preceded the coming of Christ, did it appear to men that spirit had faded away. It seemed to them the illusion of a forgotten past. Man's inner life appeared to arise wholly out of his physical existence, and seemed either to seed with it, or to degenerate into an unsatisfying shadow of itself.

But to His disciples and those who received Him, Christ appeared as an entirely new happening, the invasion of the world by the Divine Spirit itself, manifest in human form. Little as they understood Him at first, they wondered more and more at His spirit-power, over the forces of nature and of evil manifest in nature, over disease and over the hearts of men and women. Even when they thought Him overwhelmed upon the

Cross, His resurrection proved to them that His spirit-power was untouched, and soon they saw, even on the Cross, the tokens that there too He reigned in spirit.

It was for them, not only a victory whose fruits they enjoyed, but one in whose conquering power they could share. For that triumphant spirit which He had brought to earth and wielded in that human personality, was now shed abroad for ever over the whole world, and freely offered to all who would receive it into his own soul. With that spirit in their hearts, they henceforth knew themselves to be spirit-beings, whose origin and kinship were not on earth, but in heaven. "We know we are of God," wrote St. John. They, too, learned to walk the earth as victors over all that world or flesh, that sin or death, might do to them. "In all things we are more than conquerors, through Him that loved us."

Nor was it only a victory for themselves as individuals. It was a victory that would wrest the world itself eventually from the powers that had dominated it. It was a spirit-impulse that entered in some measure into every human being the whole world over and to all time, by which all men might share in the victory.

\* \* \*

That is what the Easter victory can mean to each of us to-day. It all turns on the true realisation of what happened in Jesus Christ. If we see in Him merely the peak of human evolution, that may evoke in us wonder—or despair. It will not give us victory. But if we see in Him the Son of God, out of His divine love bringing to mankind the spirit-power of God Himself, a power that, as He has never left us, is always available for us, then in spite of many failures and defeats, we can live in this certainty that that spirit will always defeat the world.

"Who is he that overcometh the world, but he that believeth that Jesus Christ is the son of God?"

# SPIRIT TRIUMPHANT

Easter Day is the great Christian Feast of the Resurrection Of Jesus Christ from the grave, the manifestation of His victory over the forces of evil that had thought to destroy Him on the cross, and the deliverance of man from the haunting fear of death by the proof of immortality. That this was an actual fact of human history is the essence of the Christian gospel and is enshrined in the Christian creed; "suffered under Pontius Pilate, was crucified dead and buried... The third day He rose again from the dead." It was the living witness of men and women who had known Him in life, and seen Him die, and had seen Him alive again, that was the compelling force that spread the gospel through the Roman world. St. Paul speaks of it as evidence that should overwhelm materialistic scepticism. The detailed record of that human witness in the Gospels and its unbroken memorial in the sacramental worship of the Church has been the anchor-sheet of faith to generations of Christians.

Once again during the past week we have followed the historical details of the Passion, listening to the Gospel records and accompanying in thought and meditation the daily events, which brought us on Good Friday to the Cross itself. Tomorrow and on the following days we shall hear the strangely beautiful stories of the appearances to the disciples of the risen Christ. All will renew and quicken our faith.

But essential as it was that this great deed of Christ should be accomplished in historical form and setting, we must be aware of thinking of it only as a historical event at a particular moment of time. As such, the Resurrection would seem to be its climax, and, having followed the story to its triumphant ending, we might allow our faith to rest in this assurance of the completed work of Christ's salvation, until once more next year we renew again the re-living of the historical events. That appears to be somewhat the mind of many, whose Christian observance is almost entirely confined to the Easter Festival.

In its deepest sense Easter is not an end, but a beginning. It was the climax of the earthly story, but the beginning of the great spiritual victory it inaugurated, Spirit triumphant in the life of the individual, in the destiny of mankind, in the whole cosmic evolution of the Earth. In His resurrection Christ did not only manifest the fact that immortality is victor over death; He achieved something new, something that He alone could have accomplished. St. Paul speaks of it when he speaks of Christ as "the first-begotten from the dead", as "the first-fruits of the Resurrection", in which eventually all could share. But only "eventually", at the end of the age, for those who would lay hold of it. The Resurrection was not only a victory over the particular event of Calvary, or the universal event of the mortality of all of us. It was far more. It was the victory over all the weight of evil since Adam's fall, that had blurred in man the image of God and poisoned for man the spirit atmosphere of the Earth. It was the promise of the restoration of man to the divine image, the recovery of his lost Paradise. It was an accomplished fact in Christ, the first-fruits of the Resurrection, for He rose from the grave in human-divine perfection. At the end it would be possible for every man who was Christ's. The Resurrection was a beginning, whose promise and performance we are to realise day by day, by letting the risen Christ in us transform our being. St. Paul expresses it in these words. "If ye then be risen with Christ, seek those things that are above... For our life is hid with Christ in God."

# THE RESURRECTION

It is admitted that it was the proclamation of the resurrection of Jesus Christ that constituted the appeal of the Christian Gospel to men and women in the first century. What was its appeal? In the first place it was a declaration of the reality and richness of life after death. This was good news both to Jews and Gentiles. A belief in a future life had once been an integral part of the ancient world religions, but for hundreds of years both Jews and Greeks had lost any sense of expectation. Life beyond death had become a world of shadows.

During the century before Christ that comfortless belief had gradually passed into unbelief or, at any rate, into a doubt that the human soul could still find its way to any future life. Christ specifically countered this unbelief and doubt. "Let not your heart be troubled. Because I live, ye shall live also." Backed by the convincing evidence of those who had seen the risen Christ, this gospel met the longings of men. Not only did it answer their scepticism, but, by its proclamation of the resurrection of the body, it denied the belief that the future life was a nebulous half-existence, not to be compared with the vivid, pulsing physical life.

*　　*　　*

Saint Paul carefully demonstrated that the risen body could not be a mere repetition of the physical body, but the belief carries a deep significance. (To expound it would be beyond the scope of this short article.) Today, however, a more scientific scepticism is widespread, and very many professing Christians have no joyous hope of immortality. But there is a further significance in the gospel of the Resurrection, which Saint Paul reveals. He speaks of the Resurrection, not only as a future hope, but as a present experience. "If ye then be risen with Christ." It was an experience of the effect of the indwelling Spirit of the risen Christ in bringing about in his soul life out of death.

*　　*　　*

The real problem of resurrection is not physical death, but spiritual death. The soul of humanity was dying because of sin and loss of spiritual vision, and that was why it had lost its hope of immortality. The experience of Saint Paul was of new life in his soul "raised from the death of sin into the life of righteousness." Here was the meaning of Christ's word, "I am the resurrection and the life." In this experience he found the undying certainty of immortality. "Nothing," he said, "can ever again separate me from this life-giving love of Christ, neither things present, nor things to come, neither life nor death." "To me to live is Christ. To die can only be to be with Him."

For us to-day, for whom there is no living witness of the resurrection of Jesus Christ, this is the certain proof—the experience of the power of the risen Christ to bring life out of death, righteousness out of sinfulness, in our souls. "Christ in us, the hope of glory." It is the heart of the Easter message, the immediate realisation of the Resurrection.

# ASCENSION

The Feast of the Ascension is one that conveys very little significance to most Christian people. It is to them a commemoration of the incident of the visible exaltation of Christ before His disciples, up to and through the clouds of heaven—the Feast of the triumphant return of Christ to His Father's side, having accomplished His work of the redemption of mankind. But it carries to most people little or no significance for *mankind*, such as is apparent in Christmas, Easter or Whitsun. Indeed, the thought of the Ascension seems to remove Christ far away from the earthly domain of man, not to descend thither again until His second Coming.

But this is to miss the deep significance of the Ascension. Easter is the restoration to mankind of his true life, shattered by sin; Ascension is the restoration to him of his true home, it is "Paradise regained." "Tell My disciples," said Christ to Mary, "that I ascend unto My Father and your Father; to My God and your God." "This that He ascended," wrote St. Paul, "what does it mean but that He also descended, *that He might fill all things*." By the Ascension Earth is reunited to Heaven, for Christ has made Himself eternally one with Man and with the Earth.

\* \* \*

The modern world has lost this wonderful truth. To it the Earth is the only home of Man, and its wonders and riches men discover and master more and more. The vast universe around is an endless field of observation and speculation, interpreted only in terms of material phenomena, and apparently utterly irrelevant to man and his destiny.

In the Middle Ages this earth-centred view of man's existence never held. They had no knowledge of modern astronomy, but sun, moon and stars were a manifestation to their human eyes of a vast spiritual universe to which man belonged, to which, through Christ's redeeming work, he would return and from which meanwhile there poured spiritual influences on man's earthly existence. "Christ hath ascended upon high; He hath led man's captor captive and hath given gifts unto men."

One can feel this medieval concept in the vast cathedrals and churches of those days. We all feel their wonder and their beauty, but when we contrast them with the ordinary dwelling-houses of those days, it seems all the more amazing that men should have erected for the worship of God such vast and towering buildings. They were shrines not only of earth, but of heaven; a whole cosmos of space and light made into a shrine for the Divine Presence, man's prayers and praises soaring to the high-flung vaulted spaces, the blessings of heaven pouring down upon the lowly worship of earth, even as the light streamed through the many-coloured windows.

\* \* \*

That is the message of the Ascension, heaven and earth reunited by the deed of Christ, Whose Presence ranges ceaselessly from the Father's side to the altars of our churches and cathedrals, and to our human hearts. This is no setting of eternity in terms of earthly space and time, but a foretaste of the eternal realities of space and time, released from their earthly limitations. As the Collect for Ascension Day expresses it, we can already by faith have this experience. "We may also in heart and mind thither ascend and with Him continually dwell."

# THE LAW OF LIBERTY

It sounds like a contradiction in terms: surely the two are opposed. You are either subject to law—or you are free. St. James doesn't seem to think so. "The law of liberty," he says, "is the perfect law." He also says it is something you "look into." He is talking about the danger of being a hearer of the word and not a doer, "deceiving your own self." To use an expressive but rather vulgar modern phrase, "Kidding yourself"— kidding yourself that because you know all about Christianity, you are "good."

That, he says, is to be like a man who looks into a mirror—a sort of magic mirror—in which he sees the likeness of the man he was meant to be, his true nature as a child of God. He sees it and acknowledges it. "That is the sort of man I have got to be," he says. Without any compulsion he freely makes it the law of his life. Then, after all that, he goes away and forgets completely what the mirror showed him. But the man who freely chooses the law of his true being never forgets what he saw, but lives it out in his life, that is the really happy man, the really *free* man

*　*　*

What is the mirror which reveals the perfect law of liberty? It is the face of Jesus Christ. In it you see reflected the face of God—and also the face of your true self. And you see for yourself that goodness is the absolute law of true being. But there is no compulsion in this law that the mirror reveals. Pictures don't compel. It can only be a law for you if you choose it freely. That is one reason why the perfect law is the law of liberty. Another reason is because it sets you free from a captivity you had never realised. Baron von Hugel, that great Christian thinker, once wrote, "I saw young fellows all around me fretting to be free, to be their own masters. They thought that if they could only get away from this thing, from that person, they would indeed be free. To me that did not seem enough. I felt I had to be free, not from anything *outside* me, but from myself, my poor, shabby, all-spoiling self. There lay freedom." That is the freedom of the mirror, the vision of your true self, what you were meant to be, reflected in the mirror of the face of Christ. If you see it and choose it freely and live by it, then you are a really free man.

*　*　*

One more unique thing about this perfect law of liberty is that if you don't live by it you lose it altogether. If you don't live it out, you will forget it altogether, you will forget you ever saw it, you will forget the magic mirror itself, the mirror of the true likeness of God and man in the face of Jesus Christ, you will forget the sort of man you were meant to be. Then your only self will be that poor lower self and you will be in bondage to it again, just as though Christ had never set you free. What greater tragedy could there be?

# A PRACTICAL MYSTERY

If there is one thing in the Christian faith which arouses the antagonism of the ordinary man, it is the doctrine of the Trinity. What can such a subtle doctrine have to do with the human agonies and perplexities of the days in which we live? I want to try to show quite shortly how utterly relevant this strange-sounding doctrine is to our deepest human needs.

There are three problems of life which have always puzzled man. To-day he is more than ever bewildered by them. The first problem is that of man's relation to the world in which he lives. It is an ancient problem and was stated in words familiar to most of us over two thousand years ago. "When I consider the heavens, the work of Thy fingers, the moon and the stars which Thou hast ordained; what is man?" To-day we are more than ever bewildered by the light which modern science has thrown upon the world. Because the world has become too complicated for our fathers' simple conception of "creation", we have lost the Creator and are ourselves more "lost" than ever.

*     *     *

In the midst of this general perplexity, however, it is well to remember that some of the greatest scientific thinkers of our day have declared that their own discoveries compel them to posit behind the visible world an Eternal Mind, in regard to which our human minds are somewhat of the same patterns. But Jesus went much further than this. Even in regard to the world of nature he bade men see God, not only as the creator of its form and fashion, but also of its wonder and beauty. "Behold the lilies of the field arrayed with a glory beyond that of Solomon." But to man He is more than this. He is the Father of men and each man is the object of His eternal love and care. In this relationship man will discover the meaning of his place in the world. "Your heavenly Father knows all your needs. Seek your true relation to Him as Creator and Father and all the rest will fall into place. Trust Him and see." The first of this Trinity of Persons, God the Maker of heaven and earth, the Father Almighty, is the answer to man's first problem.

Man's second problem is in the sphere of human history and the events of our day have made it more acute. What is the meaning of history with its ever-recurring rise and fall of nations and civilisations Are we getting anywhere? Where is the pattern and what is the goal? What does it all mean to me or to any other individual?

*     *     *

Here again, God has given the answer to our problem and given it in Himself. In the person of Jesus of Nazareth God entered the realm of human history, in closest experience of its tragic facts of sin and hatred, with purpose and power to redeem and restore. In Him past history has significance and future history has purpose. So in the second Person of the Trinity, God the Son, the Saviour of Mankind and the Lord of human life, man's second need is met.

The third problem is more than ever a modern one. It confronts us all all the time. It is the problem of our inner life of thought and feeling, of our temptations, our hopes and ideals, our good intents and our bitter failures. We all know in ourselves that here the trouble really lies, that the inconsistency of our inner life is the root cause of the unhappiness and ineffectiveness of our outer life of action. Again, through Jesus Christ, God has revealed Himself to that despair as the Holy Spirit, the Indwelling God. Who will come in to that inner life where no one else can come, and give it strength and order and wholeness, not only for this life, but as a basis for an eternal existence. Here again we find our answer in the third Person of the Trinity, God the Holy Spirit, the Strengthener, the Lord and Life-giver.

* * *

So by God's answer to three of man's deepest problems we are brought round to the Church's ancient dogma. "I believe in One God who is three Persons, Father, Son and Holy Spirit, a Trinity in Unity and a Unity in Trinity." Remember, I have only touched upon this great dogma, and have in no way exhausted or explained it. I believe that a deeper understanding of it would lift the whole human race to a higher level of thinking and living. But if we are to turn to God in these days, it must be to a God who has revealed Himself as the answer to our deepest problems. The actual discovery of the effectiveness of the answer can only be found by each one of us in an act of personal faith and adventure.

# THE EVER-PRESENT CHRIST

From one point of view Easter appears as the victorious climax of the Incarnation, the earthly life of Christ. It was His act of triumph over the powers of evil and of death, that had seemed to overwhelm Him just as they appear to overwhelm with inescapable force all human life. So to many Christians Easter appears as the triumphant conclusion of the Incarnation, and Christ as the great victor who returned with His victorious laurels to the spirit world, where after this earthly life they look to meet Him. Their prayers and thoughts are directed to Him as in heaven, sitting at the right hand of God, as one who will return to the earth only at His second coming at the end of earthly history.

There are in our creeds and liturgical prayers and hymns many phrases and sayings that confirm this point of view. On the other hand there is much in the New Testament that presents quite a different picture. All pictures in terms of earthly space and time experience can never be taken as complete expressions of spiritual existence, though it is undeniable that even theologians have fallen into the mistake of doing this. It is an error which is doubly dangerous when we fall into it in our thoughts of the risen Christ, for it robs us of the awareness of the ever-present Christ, which is the unique hope and strength of the Christian outlook, and the true significance of the Resurrection.

It was St. Paul who most clearly revealed this essential quality of the Christian faith. Through Christ the Kingdom of Heaven came down manifestly into earthly human existence, but it did not depart again at the end of Christ's earthly life. Christ's resurrection and ascension were not the end of a momentary flash of the spirit world into the life of humanity, but the beginning of a much more intense and universal spiritual presence.

"If I had known Christ in His physical life," exclaimed St. Paul, "that knowledge would mean nothing to me any more. For I know Him now in a far deeper and more wonderful experience—as Christ in me, the hope of glory." So he speaks of Christ's ascension not, as it appears on the surface in St. Luke's account of it, as a departure, with the promise of a distant return, but as the expansion of that victorious risen life throughout the whole created universe, from the throne of God at the summit of all hierarchical levels of heavenly existence, down to the level of earthly consciousness, and even below that, to what St. Paul calls "the lower parts of the earth"—those earth-bound, self-centred levels of being to which man can sink. Through and into them all He penetrates, with His triumphant risen life, "that He might fill all things," and transform them by His eternal presence in and with them.

It is this miracle of Christ's eternal unbroken presence in our earthly life, in the immediate circumstances of our daily experience, as well as in the vast uncertainties of world future, which to-day stir our hearts with fear that is the real peace and strength of the Christian life.

"Christ is always near you," said St. Paul. "In nothing be anxious, but bring to Him your longings and your fears. And a peace that is greater than all earthly wisdom will fill your heart."

# OBEYING THE VISION

"Wherefore, O King Agrippa, I was not disobedient to the heavenly vision." The story of the trial of St. Paul before Festus and Agrippa, in the twenty-sixth chapter of the Acts of the Apostles, is one of the most dramatic scenes in the Bible. It is a snapshot of the reaction of humanity to spiritual reality.

On the one hand we have Festus, the representative of material power and hard-headed scepticism, and Agrippa, the worldly, unscrupulous, licentious king whose traditions and ancestry and—sometimes—his conscience denied him the refuge of complete unbelief; and, on the other hand, you have Paul, physically insignificant and in fetters, defending his life. He begins with eloquence and persuasion, but suddenly he makes a statement which shatters the complacent attention of his judges. "As a young man", he said, "on my way to Damascus I saw, in a vision, Jesus Christ, and He told me what my life work was to be. Since then I have lived in obedience to that vision."

The reaction of the hard-headed sceptic was immediate. "The fellow is brilliant, but mad!" When Paul turned from him to pierce the troubled uncertainty which he could see in Agrippa's face, the King laughed it off. "You seem to want to make me a Christian in a few minutes!" he said. They did not want to hear any more.

\* \* \*

Mankind has always had a dread of spirit reality. Even when it seems to force itself upon us, we try to forget it, to live as though it had never happened to us. Yet Jesus deliberately challenged men with the face that He had brought them face to face with spirit reality. "If I had not done among you", he said, "the works that none other man did, you would not have had sin; but now you have no cloak for your sin."

Jesus knew, of course, that it was their very sin that was the real cause of their unbelief. Remember the words that He put in the mouth of Abraham in His parable when Dives begs Abraham to send Lazarus back to earth that he may bring conviction to Dives' brethren: "They have Moses and the prophets", said Abraham, "let them hear them". "Nay Father Abraham, but if one went unto them from the dead, they will repent." "If they hear not Moses and the prophets, neither will they be persuaded though one rose from the dead."

When a man deliberately rejects the appeal to his moral consciousness, he will reject or evade any other revelation of spirit reality. There is in the beginning of the Epistle the Hebrews a great deal about the intimate connection between sin and unbelief. It speaks of the "deceitfulness of sin," which breeds "an evil heart of unbelief in turning aside from the living God."

\* \* \*

Many people to-day try to discount all morality as an unconscious acceptance of social standards. That point of view seems to avoid the fact that man is always challenging social standards on moral grounds. As a matter of fact, conscience, the moral instinct, is itself an awareness—albeit an unconscious awareness—of the objective reality of right and wrong in the spirit world. The man who deliberately denies his moral instincts will deny all spirit reality.

There is a danger to-day in the fact that many people are seeking and professing to find evidence of spirit reality, without expecting that reality to have any effect at all on their way of living. All they surmise about is whether the evidence is convincing and whether they can get further revelations. It is a terribly dangerous situation. Either their indifference to morality will deaden their spirit perception, or it will lead it into distortion and self-deception. That was why, in the ancient Mysteries, every would-be initiate had to subject himself to a long period of moral probation.

\* \* \*

The only way to maintain our spirit perceptions and convictions is to *obey* them, to live them out in daily practice. We do not all get actual spirit vision, but spirit reality is brought home to us in countless ways, through our conscience, through sorrow, through tragedy, in prayer or meditation or worship. These "intimations of immortality" are few and far between. They can easily be overwhelmed by the ceaseless manifestations of physical reality on all sides of us. The only way of maintaining the freshness and certainty of our spirit perceptions is to obey them—and to keep on obeying them.

"How Master," asked one of the disciples, "shall we have an awareness of the presence of the Holy Spirit, which is denied to the world?" "If a man love me", replied Jesus, "he will *keep my word*—and then it will happen to him." "Wherefore I was not disobedient to the heavenly vision."

# WROUGHT BY PRAYER

There can be no question that in His teaching Jesus Christ laid the greatest emphasis on the necessity of prayer in human life. Moreover, by His own example He enforced His teaching, for He Himself often spent hours of the night in prayer. In spite of this, men and women of to-day find the greatest difficulty in making prayer a habit and even in reconciling it with a reasoned attitude towards life.

Two causes have contributed to this: first, the commonly accepted belief that everything happens according to natural law—by which is understood material cause and effect—and that therefore prayer can produce no result; and, second, the egoistic attitude which regards prayer as an activity for securing our own needs and desires. But prayer has a far wider application and purpose than petition, and it is not too much to say that, without it, no real religious life is possible.

I want to deal shortly with one aspect of prayer—with prayer as an antidote to the sense of frustration and anxiety which life often brings to the thoughtful man. In regard to this the Gospel tells us that Jesus taught men "that they ought always to pray and not to faint"—i.e., "not to be dismayed". There are two aspects of life that often confront us with a sense of discouragement and frustration.

On the one hand the past makes us discouraged—our own past, the realisation that we are far from being what we might have been and that the higher levels of life seem now to be beyond our attainment. If that despair seizes us, the remedy for it is prayer, the realisation that we are not creatures of the temporal moment, but are beings of eternity and that just as our past is not over and done with, so it is also not beyond healing and saving, and that for that very purpose Christ lived and died and rose again among men.

The other frustration which often assails us is when we look at the future with all its uncertainties. Multitudes of men and women to-day are beset by fear and anxiety for the future, and to most of them prayer seems useless and irrelevant. Such an attitude is really rather unintelligent. It is surely plain that events are not settled only by material causes, but also by the reaction of men and women to their outward circumstances. A certain school of thought may tell us that every one of our actions is pre-determined by our past, but the average man does not feel it to be true.

He feels that he can confront a situation with a certain independence of his past, and can make an original decision. He is right.

The human will, if it becomes aware of it, can be an *originator* of action. In prayer the Christian can lift himself above the flux of time and material causation and can unite his spirit with the divine creative spirit of Christ, by which all things can be made new. Through prayer he finds that he can face with equanimity whatever the future may bring. It can be a matter of easily proved experience that we confront our lot or fate quite differently when we have prepared for it by prayer than when we have only shrunk from it in fear.

          \*          \*          \*

Man is a spirit being living under physical conditions for a spiritual end of eternal importance; but it is fatally easy for him to lose sight of the end by treating the means as though they themselves were the end. That is what our age is suffering from. Prayer is the first step in the conscious lifting of our spirit out of the flux of physical existence into the reality of spirit life. Its primary condition is faith, faith awakened in us by the life and teaching of Jesus Christ as recorded in the Gospels, and quickened by spiritual experience. Prayer is the response of our will to that faith, the conscious and deliberate contemplation of our-self and our day-by-day life in their true spiritual setting. Beyond prayer lie higher realms of spiritual experience and discovery, *but prayer is the first step*, without which the others can never be attained.

In this Rogation Week falls the great feast of the Ascension. This visible act of Christ was not merely for the purpose of showing to His disciples that He had finally left the sphere of the earth life, but also to show that before their eyes He had passed to that life of the spirit to which they, too, belonged, and in which they could still find Him. In the words of the Ascension Collect, we pray "that we also in heart and mind thither ascend and with Him continually dwell" That is the heart and essence of prayer.

# THE INDWELLING SPIRIT

Whitsun is the Festival of the Holy Spirit, the great gift of God to man through Jesus Christ. Many people find it hard to understand what is meant by "the coming of the Holy Ghost". Had not the Spirit of God come to man before? What is the relation of the Holy Spirit of Pentecost to the Spirit of God of Whom we read in the Old Testament? The difference is not that of "wrath" and "love"—the Spirit of wrath manifest in Sinai's thunderings and the Spirit of dove-like love manifest in Jesus Christ. The difference is that the Spirit of the Old Testament came to men from *without* and the Spirit of the New Testament from *within*.

In ancient days men were more directly aware of the reality of the unseen world, as we see in the beginning of the Old Testament and even to-day in simpler forms of civilisation. But gradually this spirit vision faded, except in a few, the prophets and seers, and they felt that the inspiration which came to them was through some divine power which laid hold of them from without and compelled obedience. But by the time of Christ prophetic vision had failed, the ancient Mysteries were corrupted, and mankind seemed cut off from the spirit world.

\* \* \*

Jesus Christ brought a new way from God to man, the way of man's heart, of inner life. Not only did Jesus manifest God to man in outward deed and word, but in His own inner life, in the life of His soul He realised in Himself the perfect relationship between God and man. God was incarnate in the physical life of Jesus, and in His soul life the Holy Spirit was ensouled.

By His love for them He awakened love and devotion in the souls of His disciples and in their oneness with Him the Holy Spirit, which lived in His own soul, was imparted to them. "The Comforter whom the Father will send in my name." "If a man love me he will keep my words and we will come unto him and make our abode with him." It was the realisation of the vision of Jeremiah. "I will put my law in their inward parts and in their heart I will write it." In their love for their Master the disciples felt the Holy Spirit come to life within them, guiding and empowering them from within. It was indeed "the Spirit of Jesus."

\* \* \*

Man's great need to-day is the redemption of his inner life, his soul life, his life of thought and desire. It is a great tragedy of our time that men are indifferent to the quality of their inner life, thinking that it is of no importance unless it is expressed in action. Yet in reality that inner life, the life of our soul, we shall take with us through death. Moreover, the life of action is derived from it, for good or evil. A man is defiled, said Jesus, by what proceeds out of his heart.

The only way in which to redeem our inner life is to unite it with the life of Christ in love and loyalty and devotion and by prayer and deliberate meditation to open our life of thought and desire to Christ, to admit Him to the very sanctuary of our being. In that union we shall find

48

that our inner life is changed and that the Spirit which lives in the soul of Jesus is at work in us. It is a matter of discovery and experience. "In that day ye shall know that I am in my father and ye in me and I in you." In these words Jesus explained to his disciples the coming of the Holy Ghost.

*    *    *

This experience is not only, nor chiefly, a solitary experience. Just as it arises in fellowship between our souls and Christ, so, too, it is fostered and grows by fellowship with one another. But it must be a real fellowship, not merely being together in one place. It must be a fellowship of soul, a fellowship of common devotion to Christ and of love to one another. These are not mere conventional expressions of religious piety; they are the laws of the Spirit, in obedience to which there awaits for any of us the discovery within ourselves of the indwelling Spirit of God.

# ASCENSION-WHITSUN-TRINITY

The three last festivals of the Church's year follow one another so swiftly in the space of two and a half weeks that one may wonder why they are so crowded and fail to see their intimate relationship as the highest peak of Christian revelation. The life and death of Christ were over, and in the victory of His resurrection He had banished forever the fear that man is only a creature of space, whom death annihilates; and had revealed to him the indestructibility of that inner soul-existence of which he is conscious, yet finds so fugitive and uncertain. Yet still the scene of Christ's action was directed earthwards, to the human soul-life of His apostles, to whom He showed Himself alive and whom He taught truths of the spirit that only now their hearts could comprehend.

Suddenly the scene expands from earth to the pure spirit realm of man's true being. "In their sight He ascended up into Heaven." The description of that last physical manifestation is applied with too literal concepts, as of a material body that can only be in one place at a time, as though Christ, having ascended, has left the earth for His seat at the right hand of God. But Saint Paul in his Epistle to the Ephesians gives the true picture. "For that He ascended, what does it imply bur that He descended, even to the lower parts of the earth, that He might fill all things." In the spirit world movement is not a change of location, but the expansion of consciousness and activity. The divine-human being of

49

Christ, which had been manifest in physical form, is now exalted to fill the whole realm of being from the physical to the divine.

And from this realm of man's true being He poured down its spiritual faculties and potentialities. "He ascended up on high and gave gifts unto men." Not only, for a while, the strange unearthly gifts of diverse tongues of power over sickness and the evil forces of nature, but above all like a sea engulfing them the downpouring of that divine love which is the foundation of spirit being, "the love of God shed abroad in our hearts through the Holy Ghost." Not only deliverance from the taint of our earthly past, and from the fear of the certain end of death, but now a foretaste of our true being and existence.

"Because ye are sons of God, God hath sent forth the spirit of His son into your hearts."

Finally, with that foretaste of heaven in the gifts of the spirit, our vision is lifted up beyond ourselves and our earthly existence to the mystery of the Godhead itself. Trinity Sunday is not the feast of an incomprehensible dogma, but a vision of the source and fount of our Redemption which is expressed to us in the Mystery of the Trinity in Unity; or as Christ Himself spoke it: "I in them and Thou in me, that they may be perfected into the one." It is the crowning vision of the Christian revelation.

> *God Almighty and with Him*
> *Cherubim and Seraphim,*
> *Filling all eternity.*
> *Adonai Elohim!*

# THE CHALLENGE OF LOVE

On Trinity Sunday the Church bids us think of the Being and Nature of God in the form of a great mystery. "God is Trinity in Unity, Three Persons in One God." The very next Sunday the Being of God is defined for us in the words that seem absolutely simple and comprehensible. "God is Love." Many people say: "That is the whole gospel and it is profoundly simple: God is Love. The love of God is all that matters; we need not concern ourselves with the bewildering doctrine of the Trinity. Love God who loves us, and the rest looks after itself." But it is not so simple as that. After all, do most Christians feel that they love God as St. Paul and St. John did?

Is there, then, any deeper connection between the explanation of the Being of God in the terms of that strange and incomprehensible doctrine of the Trinity in Unity, and this apparently simple, yet deeply mysterious definition, "God is Love"? One is an explanation in terms of God's own divine Being; the other is in terms of His relationship to man. Yes, there is a relationship between these two definitions, and it was set out by the Being most qualified to interpret them both, Jesus Christ Himself. In that wonderful last prayer before His Passion, He speaks about the mystery of the Divine Trinity in the most explicit terms. In fact it is the only explicit reference to this doctrine in the New Testament.

These are His words: "I pray that they all may be one"—and the Greek word there means oneness of being—"even as Thou, Father, art in me and I in Thee, that they also may be in us. ...I in them, and Thou in me, that they may be perfected into one. Father Thou lovest me before the foundation of the world, and I made known unto them Thy name, that the love wherewith Thou lovest me may be in them, and I in them."

There the doctrine of the Trinity in Unity is revealed as the eternal love between the Father and the Son before time was, and that love, proceeding from them both, is itself spirit, Father Son and Holy Spirit, an eternal Trinity constituting the unity of the Godhead. And this profound mystery is not something aloof from man: man's destiny is to participate in it — "that they may be one, even as we are one, that the love wherewith Thou lovest me may be in them."

There lies the difficulty. For the love of which St. John speaks is very different from what we call love. It is not emotion, but devotion; not feeling but deeds. Not what you give because you expect it to be returned, but what you give for the sake of giving it, whether you receive it back or not—giving it simply to awaken the spirit of love in the other. This love, says St. John, did not begin with us, it began with God, in giving His Son for our salvation, when we neither knew nor loved Him. It is that amazing, unchangeable love of God for me, no matter what I am, that is my only way to discover true love.

But though divine love begins with God, man's response to it must begin by loving his fellow-men. It is when we love each other—and all others—with the same love that we have seen God has towards ourself, that we shall arrive at loving God Himself.

"If we love one another," St. John tells us, "God dwelleth in us and we in God." It is the mystery of man lifted into unity with the Divine

51

Trinity. But it begins with the simple practical message of God, that he who would love God in this way must first love his fellow-men.

# JOHN THE BAPTIST

John the Baptist, whose Nativity Festival falls to-day is one of the most enigmatic and potent figures in history, but his lustre was dimmed because it was so immediately outshone by the greater light of which he was the herald. John spoke truly when he said: "He must increase but I must decrease." But in John's darkest hour of doubt and apparent failure Jesus spoke about him in words that suggest a spiritually gigantic figure, whose stature towers above the world's dim realisation. "Of all men born of women, none is greater than John," he declared and he bewildered his hearers' limited comprehension by identifying John with that other enigmatic figure of their history, Elijah, whose reincarnation was an expectation of Messianic prophecy. Whether or not Jesus's words pointed to a spiritual reality, of which the Jews—and even John himself—were obviously unaware, the parallel, in almost every detail, between the character and history of those two strange figures is an arresting fact, and must carry a deeper significance than that of similarity.

\* \* \*

Moreover against John's overwhelming, but short-lived popularity, Jesus reveals two weaknesses in the popular approach to religion, which apply to our own age just as much as to that of Christ's hearers. "What did you flock out into the wilderness to see?" he asked them. "A nine-days wonder? Or a man who would justify your own worldly ways to yourselves? Or a man speaking to you with the mouth of God? If the last, then his message is still your concern, whatever his fate may be." It is a challenge to all those who flock to popular preachers or churches. What do you expect to find? For what is really being offered to you will remain a challenge to you for ever, even when the voice of the preacher is stilled. To respond to the attraction of a really spiritual appeal can never be dismissed as an interesting past experience or treated as an event at which you have merely been a spectator. To all eternity its spiritual challenge will confront your assent or refusal.

\* \* \*

Again in the attitude of the Jews to John and to himself Jesus revealed how the refusal to face a spiritual challenge cloaks itself in captious criticism. "John," he said, "preached to you as a stern ascetic, and you said, 'The fellow is mad. He doesn't live like other men.' I speak to you out of a common experience, as one who shares the ordinary life of men, and you say, 'Who is he to talk? He is no better than we are. He enjoys life, not like John!' You have the mind of petulant children, determined to grumble."

And the fault goes deeper than petulance. For the attitude of criticism can all to easily blind a man to spiritual reality. The man who wishes to avoid a spiritual challenge always takes refuge in criticism, and as soon as he does so his eyes are blinded and the door to his heart is barred.

# A CONTRADICTION IN TERMS

The gulf between Christianity and industry has long been a problem to the Churches. An exhaustive historical report, covering the last four centuries, has just been produced on *The National Church and the Social Order*. The problem is very often conceived as a gulf between the clergy and the workers in industry. The Vicar of Warwick wrote about that last week. That is an age-long cleavage, going back to the *Canterbury Tales*, and to the Pharisees and the tax-gatherers of Christ's day.

Another approach is the supposed gulf between professing Christians as a body and industrial workers. But after all, almost all Christians are themselves engaged in industry, so that they stand in both camps. The fact that they do so little to reconcile them arises from the fact that the conflict is not settled in themselves.

That is the whole point. The gulf between Christianity and industry is that they represent two quite different world-concepts. Christianity teaches that man and the world are spiritual in origin, in the laws by which they exist, and their destiny. Science teaches that their origin and the laws of their being are material, and the destiny of man beyond death so uncertain as to afford no interpretation of his existence.

Now, this contradiction has only arisen in the last four centuries, but to-day it asserts itself right from our schooldays. The Scripture lesson teaches us that God called Abraham and spake by the prophets. The history lesson will have none of it. It is an anthropomorphic projection of man's awakening psychic intuitions. The Scripture lesson gives Christ's teaching that the death of a sparrow and the beauty of Nature imply spiritual participation and awareness. Biology and botany will have none of it. They are merely natural events with no relation to anything outside sense-experience. And so on. And the Scripture lesson is only one half-hour in the day, or perhaps one period in the week, while all the other lessons are based on natural-scientific thinking. The Christian boy or girl comes to feel that the Incarnation was the one divine irruption into a purely natural world order, and that religion is really concerned with another world.

Then he goes into industry. It is far from being all evil or corrupting. If he has brains and ambition, it is exciting and absorbing and calls for all his skill and energy. But it is materialistic. It has nothing to do with his religious convictions—if he still retains them. It is run on other principles and has other aims, and he spends six-sevenths of his time absorbed in it. Soon he comes to think that the other seventh would be better spent in making him more fit for his real task than in maintaining a perplexing contradiction. But he is not really satisfied.

If however, anyone tries to point out that the materialistic assumptions of science are wrong, that the world is spiritual, and that there are forces and processes at work in it that are necessary to its well-being and understanding, though they are not immediately apparent to normal physical consciousness, even the religious leaders murmur, "Occultism! Wishful thinking! Surely science has disproved all this!" The only wistful doubters of scientific certainty seem to be some of the leading scientists.

Man's relations to man will never be lifted from expediency to moral certainty, except on a spiritual understanding of the visible universe. Until man's thinking is redeemed from materialism, the gulf between Christianity and the secular order will remain unbridged.

# THE SERVITUDE OF SIN

In the sixth chapter of the Epistle to the Romans—which in the Prayer Book is appointed as the Epistle for to-morrow—St. Paul speaks of life as a choice of masters. We are either the servants of God or the servants of sin. It is not unnatural to regard goodness as obedience to the law of God, but we do not usually regard sin as obedience to some "other," but as doing what we like. But St. Paul insists that sin is not merely an abstract concept of certain tendencies in human behaviour, arising out of man himself, but that it is the expression of the conscious will of spirit beings, making an attack upon the will of man and woman. Just as in goodness we offer ourselves to be instruments of the will of God, so in sin we "present our members as instruments," through which the will of evil spirit beings is done.

It is so widely assumed that our impulses, our temptations and our desires spring up within us, that even theologians to-day teach that belief in the devil is outworn. It is a most dangerous isolation of man from the spirit world.

After all when we look more closely, sin *has* the appearance of servitude. In the first place there is little that is "original" in sin We all sin in the same ways; most sins are common to most men. It certainly looks like some great external pattern expressing itself in us.

Ironically enough, when someone does sin in an original way, we say that he is "possessed by a devil!" Again, the more we indulge in a sin, the less it satisfies us and seems to be the real expression of us, and yet the more helpless we are to get free form it. That looks like servitude.

St. Paul carries the argument further by speaking of the consequences of sin. "The wages of sin is death." "Wages" implies a personal relationship and an intentional and inevitable reward of sin—in spiritual death. But just as the true nature of sin is hidden from us, so is its reward.

*　　*　　*

This conception of sin as servitude to the spirit forces of evil is not a denial of human free will, but a challenge to it. If sin is our free choice, it may excuse itself as the right to self-expression. But if it is in reality a servitude to evil powers, who will reward the sinner only with spiritual death, then it becomes a challenge to man's free will to enlist in a counter-offensive. To this service he can only be loyal by acts of free will so continuously disciplined that they wear the appearance of acts of obedience. Yet increasingly these acts become the expression of himself and this service of God becomes his freedom—a freedom which brings a reward so incommensurate that it can only be described as a royal bounty. "The wages of sin is death, but the free gift of God is eternal life."

# IS THE DEVIL REAL?

"Then was Jesus led up into the wilderness to be tempted of the devil." The temptation of Our Lord is the one incident recorded in the Gospels which no other person could have witnessed but Christ Himself and concerning which no account could have been derived except from His own lips. That fact lends a unique importance and significance to the account of this event.

I was at a clerical discussion group some time ago when a dignitary of the Church suddenly said to me: "Do you really believe in a personal devil?" Of course, "personal" is a somewhat loose expression, but I knew what he meant. Did I really believe that evil found actual expression in a being of the spirit world whose relation to mankind is that of a tempter, one who actively seeks to divert man from the attainment of God's purpose for him? Was not sin and evil simply the measure of man's own limitations and imperfections on the pathway of physical and moral evolution, and the deformity of his will only the result of his past wrong choices?

\*　　\*　　\*

I replied to my questioner that I certainly did believe in a personal devil. So did Jesus Christ. So far from explaining away the devil in terms of human frailty, Jesus saw, in the not-unnatural refusal of His disciple to accept for Him the possibility of disaster and shameful death, a subtle temptation of Himself by the devil. "Get thee behind me, Satan!" St. Paul, too, believed in the devil: "Our wrestling is not against flesh and blood."

All the psychologising away of the personal spiritual reality of evil is due to the fact that humanity has become increasingly unaware of and incredulous about the existence of the spirit world, owing to the entire pre-occupation of scientific thought with physical reality. Christian thought has been to a great extent affected by scientific concepts.

Of course if the evil in man is to be entirely explained as originating in himself in the process of his physical evolution, then the good in him must be similarly explained. My questioner would never have suggested that, for it is a heresy. But that logical conclusion has been arrived at by very many people—and it is exactly what the devil foresaw. There could have been no cleverer move on the part of the powers of evil than to make man believe that they themselves had no real existence. Nothing makes attack easier than to persuade your enemy that you are not there.

\*　　\*　　\*

It was only a couple of decades after man had discarded his belief in the reality of the devil that he began to discard his belief in the reality of God. A couple more decades past and brought man to the stage when, in face of the desolation of world-wide war and the crumbling of human civilisation, he began to lose faith in himself as a being of any absolute worth and saw himself only as an item in a physical evolution, which seemed itself to have no spiritual or moral significance and left none for him. It was a logical sequence of disbelief.

The fundamental temptation of our age has been the belief that there is no reality beyond the material and no history of man outside the range of the physical. Such a belief takes the heart out of religion, for how can man see any real need for atonement or have any real zest for spiritual struggle in a mere process of physical evolution? He tends to regard himself with complacence or self-pity or mere disgust, according as his lot is easy or difficult or utterly desperate.

*    *    *

But to feel that the moral issues of life are a matter of a spirit warfare, in which man himself is called and empowered of God to take sides and play a real part, and in which he knows that the whole resources of God are on his side, brings to life zest and watchfulness and effort. A man sees evil as an actual spiritual assault on his being and though he does not excuse himself for yielding to it, he does not feel that it is an essential part of himself. From that he gains sympathy and generosity towards the failings of others, even of his bitterest enemies.

Moreover, he is able to see the hideous depravities which have darkened the recent history of mankind, not as an evolutionary retrogression which makes him despair of the future of man, but as a desperate assault of evil, which inspires him to a more active and determined co-operation with the yet stronger and always available forces of spiritual goodness.

# FATHER AND CHILD

When Christ's disciples asked Him to teach them to pray, He replied, "When ye pray, say, 'Our Father.'" The words are so familiar to us, the prayer is so familiar to us, that we often use it very superficially. "The Fatherhood of God" is often glibly uttered as being the broad basis of Christianity, a sort of belief that everyone can accept. Yet there is no realisation of the profound significance which attaches to those so familiar words. "Our Father."

They must have startled the disciples, for though their scriptures often spoke of God being like a father, yet very rarely did they speak of Him as their father, and never in that direct way. Indeed the Pharisees were indignant with Jesus for calling God "His Father," "thus," said they, "making Himself equal with God." That is the deep significance of these words. To pray to God as "Our Father" is not only to claim His love and care and protection, but is to make a claim for ourselves. If God is our

Father, then we are His sons and daughters, partakers of His very nature. It is an assertion that in our deepest self we are not of this world, but that we derive our nature from God, and that, in that profound way, He is our Father.

*     *     *

This sublime fact is lost sight of in the theological statement that we are not "by nature" children of God, but only by "adoption." This uses the word "adoption" in the modern sense, which implies taking, as your own child, one that was not yours before, but the child of other parents. But "adoption," in the Roman world, and as St. Paul uses it in his Epistle to the Galatians, means something quite different.

He explains quite plainly in the fourth chapter that he is referring to the custom of putting a child in his early years under the tutelage of slaves, and "though he is lord of all"—his father's heir—treating him on the servant level. But at a certain age his father releases him from that position and gives him the status and recognition of that sonship which had really always been his.

The parallel in St. Paul's mind was the release from servitude to the Jewish law, which he saw was only a temporary condition, to the freedom of revealed and recognised sonship to God, through Jesus Christ. The contrast between "children of wrath" and "children of grace" is not a contrast between two different natures, but between two different conditions, under which the children of God may be living.

The newly-recognised status of sonship is made possible for us only by grace, that is by the free gift of the deed of Christ. Owing to our sins, we, the children of God, are also "children of wrath," that is, subject to the inevitable moral consequences of our sins, declared by the Moral Law. But by the grace of Christ we have been set free—if we will accept it—from the inevitability of that moral consequence, and restored to the freedom of our revealed true nature, as "children of God, our heavenly Father."

"Because we *are* sons," writes St. Paul, "God hath sent forth the Spirit of His Son into our hearts, teaching us to say 'Father.'"

It is a tremendous thought, one that we should meditate deeply, in order that we may realise all its wonder and all its demands. "If children," St. Paul adds, "then heirs; heirs of God and joint-heirs with Christ." Nothing more stupendous has ever been said, or could ever be said about man.

That tremendous status, that inconceivable heritage, belongs to all men and women. Some are still in tutelage to some lower order or constraint, in ignorance of their divine sonship. Some who have been admitted to their true status can yet throw away their heritage. But nothing can alter that sublime truth that we are in our spirit partakers of the very nature of God. So when ye pray, Christ taught us, say, "Our Father."

# THE EARTH IS THE LORD'S

At this time Harvest Thanksgiving services are being held in places of worship all over the land. There is a spontaneity in these services, for man has always instinctively felt joy and thankfulness for the bounty and beauty of Nature. But to make our thanksgiving an act of worship, there must be in it, beyond the delight in these things, a conscious relationship to God Who gives them.

No one can read the Gospels without being struck by the constant use by Christ of the rhythm in Nature of seed-time and harvest to illustrate His teaching. It was not only because these illustrations were familiar to all His hearers, but because in Nature, in this rhythm of life and death and resurrection, we have a picture in time and space, of the rhythm of man's own life in time and eternity. Not to realise this is to miss the deepest meaning in Christ's parables. Moreover in putting so great an emphasis upon this relationship of the Earth to Man, Christ reveals to us that the deepest understanding of the Earth itself is to be found in its unceasing rhythm of life and death, rather than in its immediate material manifestation—in its temporal rather than in its spatial existence.

This forms the contrast between the spiritual and the scientific approach to the Earth. Science considers the Earth from the spatial aspect, as a material object immediately manifest to man's senses, to be understood and made use of. True, science is deeply concerned with agriculture and with its processes of seed and growth, but only in their use for man, now or at some future moment of his material existence. It is not concerned with the mystery of upsurging and receding life, from root to stem, to flower and fruit and seed. It is only concerned with food values. For science, *the Earth is Man's* to know, to master, to use and to enjoy. The question whence the Earth came, or what is its destiny, or whether it has any deeper significance than its immediate material use is not the concern of the scientific approach. It lies outside the realm of sense observation and logical proof.

But the spiritual view sees in each seed-time and harvest the wonder of this rhythm of life and death, a rhythm not made by man, on which he is dependent for his very existence, and which, if he exploits it selfishly or greedily, he will distort or even destroy. It is something which man neither owns, nor can dispense with, and which he does not even fully understand. The spiritual view sees the essential being of the Earth as penetrated by this rhythm, which is of time rather than of space, and which, as in man's own being, extends in either direction beyond its immediate material existence. Thus this rhythm in which the Earth speaks to man of his own essential being, is also a witness that the Earth itself shares in that hidden time-existence. Our Harvest Thanksgivings, then, remind us that the Earth does not belong to man, but that "The Earth is the Lord's and the fulness thereof."

# MICHAEL AND ALL ANGELS

The Church of England gives one festival in her Calendar, September 29, to angels. To most Christian people angels have a vague, problematic existence and have no real place in their conception of the universe. The subject of angels has been brought into the limelight recently by the refusal of chancellor of a diocese to grant a faculty for the erection of an angel-figure on a child's grave. It has aroused a good deal of controversy on the nature of angels and man.

The ancient world regarded angelic beings as the inhabitants of the spirit world by whose co-operation with God the world came into being, and was sustained. A tendency grew up to deify and worship these beings and the monotheistic Jewish faith rebelled against this. Later the Christian faith came up against the same danger in the complicated angelic cults of the Gnostics, and gradually substituted the cult of the saints for that of the angels.

*    *    *

The best guide for our thoughts on this subject is the place which angels play in the New Testament and especially in the life and consciousness of Jesus Christ. It would seem as if, with the coming of Christ, there was an irruption of the spiritual world into human consciousness on a far greater scale than anything in Jewish history for a thousand years. This of course one would expect. There is the great Archangel of the Annunciation, Gabriel; a great host of angels announce the birth of Jesus; Jesus is strengthened in His temptation and comforted in His agony by angels, who also announce His resurrection. But Jesus Himself refers to angels quite naturally, yet quite specifically. He speaks of the guardian angels of children. He interprets one of His parables by saying "The reapers are the angels. The Son of Man shall send forth His angels." Also He speaks to Caiaphas of "the Son of Man coming on the clouds of heaven with His holy angels."

There can be no doubt that He knew the angels as a vast spiritual company, sharing and serving in His great task of the redemption of mankind. He speaks, too, of human beings in heaven living "as angels."

* * *

In these materialistic days nothing is more inspiring than the thought of this vast host of spirit beings, amongst whom is our home and origin, animated by the will of God and participating in the redemptive work of Christ for man, surrounding and interpenetrating our earthly world. There is so much of evil in the world to-day, and many too are conscious of dark spiritual forces animating this evil. It is a thought of strength and comfort to call to mind the angelic hosts who fight for the right, led by the mighty Archangel Michael, champion of the cause of God—Michael, "The countenance of Christ." Instead of thinking of a world of atoms, let us think of a world of angels, beings animated by the same love of God and loyalty to Christ as ourselves. "I am a fellow-servant with thee and with thy brethren that hold the Testimony of Jesus."

> *The Angels keep their ancient places,*
> *Turn but a stone and start a wing.*
> *Tis ye tis your estranged faces*
> *That miss the many-splendoured thing.*

## ALL SAINTS' DAY

When I wrote a month ago it was the Feast of St. Michael and All Angels. To-day it is the Feast of All Saints and our thoughts are lifted once more to the world of spirit-reality. That is good for us. In this life of materialistic preoccupation, with its perplexity of threatening and seemingly insoluble problems, it is above all things important that we should see it against the true background of its source and end. Some call this escapism, but it is nothing of the kind. Escapism is to run away from the hard facts of life into some subjective dream in which we find false comfort. But the Christian who is conscious of the spiritual world is not running away from the facts of his earthly life at all, nor is he creating an imaginary contrast. He is recalling a reality which is easily lost sight of, a reality which contains the solution of earth's problems and in the recollection of which we are most likely to find those solutions here and now: a reality which gives significance and purpose to this earthly life which to many people appears to lack either. It does not only make this life endurable, but it makes it worth living with courage and contentment. It does not only explain it or compensate for it, but it reveals that in this life's experiences are to be found the substance and foundation on which our true life in the spirit world can be built.

*     *     *

This Feast of All Saints bids us think of all those who have passed out of this world in the faith and fear of Christ, and have entered into the experience of that life which is the fruit of this. The saints are not a select company of superhumanly pious souls, but a vast host of men and women of all types and kinds. Some walked this life in natural gentleness and goodness; others fought their way through fierce temptations and frequent falls. Some were those whose lives their fellow men could not help acclaiming as noble and exalted; some were despised others were condemned for their palpable sins. Some had to pass after death through the flame of purification; others "needed not save to wash their feet." But there they are our brothers, sisters, parents, children, friends, the great and joyous company of the redeemed and on their lips is the same song: "Unto Him that loved us and loosed us from our sins and made us to be a kingdom, to Him be glory and dominion." For whether as companion and pattern in their life of holiness, or as one whose strength and forgiveness upheld them in conflict or defeat, or who plunged to the depth of their sin-polluted life and snatched them from the very clutch of Satan, they know that it is to Him in whom they learned to trust that they owe the life to which they have attained.

*     *     *

This great company of the saints do not turn their back upon this life on earth, as something from which they have escaped. No spirit redeemed by Christ can fail to have His compassionate love for the earth. The medieval instinct that lifted its cry to the saints for strength and succour was a true one and did in reality no despite to the Divine Saviour, from whom alone the love and prayer of the saints are drawn. With this thought the author of the Epistle to the Hebrews encourages us: "Seeing we are compassed about with so great a cloud of witnesses, let us run with endurance the race that is set before us."

62

# IN REMEMBRANCE

Remembrance Sunday is in the first place an act of corporate national acknowledgement of the debt we owe as a people, for our lives and for the survival of our liberties, to those in the two world wars who gave their lives for us. It is an acknowledgement that the greatest and purest achievement of those wars was human self-sacrifice. It is also a constant reminder—all the more necessary under the increasing threat of a materialistic scientific organisation of society—that the worth or cost of any situation must be measured by its effect upon the life and being of men and women.

The other side of Remembrance Sunday is our individual remembrance of our own loved ones who made that sacrifice. This brings to many a deep sadness, in looking back to the loss of a physical presence, a loss which remembrance makes all the more poignant.

But there is another aspect of remembrance, to which the Christian faith bears witness. Man's sense of Time, his power of memory, is one of the things which distinguish him from the animal. By it he becomes conscious of his being as not limited to the experience of the passing moment. Nevertheless , it brings with it a certain nostalgia. The thing which he remembers he seems to have lost. But the Christian hope of immortality is not merely of another, this time endless, existence, but of the recovery and sublimation of all earthly experience. We tend to think of this always in terms of judgement, but Christ does not only warn us that we shall have to face the moral reality of our misdeeds, open or secret, but that we shall also reap the harvest of our good deeds, our happy days. No cup of kindness, no deed of love or generosity, no true relationship, but will be harvested as a real experience. As the late Dean Inge once wrote, with that penetrating mystic realism that set him above most English theologians and philosophers, "what is negated in timelessness is not the reality of the present, but the unreality of the past and future. Time is only forbidden to devour itself."

For the Christian, remembrance of happy days of companionship with his loved ones is not a sad recollection of something lost, but a certainty that those days are imperishable and that for *them* they are already a recovered living experience, in which, in our remembrance of them, we can even now in measure share.

The command, "This do in remembrance of me," was not a means whereby Christ's disciples should not forget their Master, or should sorrowfully recollect him, but a meeting with his living presence, in which memory became once more experience, for ever delivered from the destructive corrosion of earthly time. The Eucharist is both the pledge of our immortality and the foretaste of its experience, the partaking of eternal life and the immediate communion of saints.

# BEING AND DOING

Jesus often emphasised the importance of "doing" and its necessity as the complement of "knowing". "If ye know these things, blessed are ye if ye *do* them." "He that heareth these words of mine and *doeth* them shall be likened unto a wise man." He is speaking there to men swept away with a new teaching and a new manifestation of power.

Yet He also contrasted "doing" with "being" and emphasised the primary importance of "being". "Make the tree good", He said, "and the fruit of good deeds will appear on it. It is impossible to gather grapes off a thorn bush or figs from thistles." Here He is speaking to the Jews, to whom religion was a rigorous system of "doing". The danger was that the doing should not proceed from the nature of the man, but simply be a performance. That was what Jesus condemned as hypocrisy, that their hearts, their character, had no relation to their external actions.

         \*      \*      \*

Another danger—and a real one to-day—is to be so busy *doing* things that you have no time to give for the task of *being*. We have no time for quiet, for meditation, for prayer, for self-examination and self-knowledge. Then inevitably, the quality of our doing suffers, for, like the fruit on a tree, our deeds proceed out of our *being*.

This comes out very strongly in the life of Archbishop Lang, published this week and already much discussed. It is very easy to over-emphasise the discrepancies in his character, for what are only regarded as weaknesses in a distinguished layman seem serious faults in a bishop. But Archbishop Lang himself, when in his holiday home in the Highlands he had time for uninterrupted prayer and self-examination, repeatedly lamented how poor his normal busy life was in these inner activities of the spirit and how grievously at times it suffered from this lack.

How much more will this be true in the life of most of us, occupied almost entirely with secular concerns as we are, and only too often with little or no time for prayer or consideration of ourselves and with little understanding of what is our real self. "Make the tree good", said Jesus, "and the rest will follow. Your deeds will inevitably be good, for they will follow naturally out of your being."

                \*       \*       \*

Two thoughts follow from this saying of Jesus. First, that which really matters is our inner being, our life of thought and feeling and will. Not only is it the fount of our actions, but that inner life is, in a very real sense, our true self, for it is that which survives death. It is desperately important that that inner life should be integrated, that it should be consistent in its pattern. And yet how often how chaotic it is, what a jumble of unregulated, uncontrolled thoughts and feelings we have and how little we think it matters, because, after all, it is our own concern and nobody else knows.

But it will not always be so. One day that confused, inconsistent inner life of mine will be apparent to myself and to others as the real "me". "There is nothing hid which shall not be known", Jesus warns us. "What you think is as secret as a whispered confidence shall one day be as plain as if you had shouted it from the housetop." There is nothing more urgent for us to realise to-day than this truth. It is the neglect of it that makes so much of our modern living so ineffective and unsatisfying, and it accounts for the uncertainty of our moral standards.

                \*       \*       \*

The second thought is that the tree can only be made good by conscious deliberate effort, realising the vital importance of the task before us. The first necessity is to know that inner life, that inner self, to contemplate it and judge it with utter sincerity, as though we were looking at the life of another. Just as we must *love our neighbour* as though he were ourself, so must we *judge ourself* as though we were our neighbour!

And when we really know that inner self, we shall discover that only in constant union of heart and will with Christ can it be made good and that out of its goodness our outer life of action will flow as naturally as fruits grow on a tree.

# PART TWO

## The Church and Rudolf Steiner

*"The foregoing generation beheld God and nature face to face; we, through their eyes. Why should not we also enjoy an original relation to the universe? Why should not we have a poetry and philosophy of insight and not of tradition, and a religion by revelation to us and not the history of theirs?"*

Nature by R. W. EMERSON 1836

# THE BATTLE FOR THE SPIRIT[5]

## THE COUNCIL OF CONSTANTINOPLE, 869 A.D.

In his exposition of the evolution of human consciousness Rudolf Steiner often spoke of the critical importance of the Council of Constantinople in 869 A.D. at which the Western Church officially renounced the ancient conception of man as a threefold being, of body, soul and spirit, by asserting that he is a duality of body and soul only. This article is an attempt to set out the historical background and spiritual significance of this Council. It will be seen to be a closely woven pattern of events which led up to the spiritual crisis of the ninth century.

It is impossible to understand this historical background  unless we grasp clearly the ecclesiastical atmosphere of Constantinople, the capital of the Byzantine Empire. If Rome might be considered  as the head of the Christian Church, and Antioch and Alexandria as its brain, Constantinople was its heart. Built in the first enthusiasm of Imperial Christianity as a Christian city, in which no pagan worship was to be allowed, it presented a real organic unity of Church and State. The famous Code of Justinian, by which the Empire was governed for centuries, began with an invocation of the Blessed Trinity, and was declared to be enacted in order to establish more firmly the practice of the Christian Faith. The Patriarch ranked next to the Emperor.

Another point to be borne in mind is the complete contrast between the Byzantine Empire and Western Europe, and, consequently, between Eastern and Western Christianity. The Byzantine Empire was for nearly a thousand years one of the most civilised, cultured and effectively ordered States the world has seen, while Western Europe was a welter of struggling tribal settlements, and later of rising and falling semi-barbarian kingdoms, encircling and often overwhelming the ever-diminishing remnant, in the centre of Italy, of what had once been the glory of Rome. Moreover, the Eastern Empire was in direct contact with the Persian and, from the seventh century, with the Arabian empires, in which the Aristotelian wisdom of Greece had taken root, and was manifesting itself in the most advanced forms of science, medicine and

---

5  First given as a lecture at an Anthroposophical conference and later published in the Golden Blade 1963.

astronomy. It was in consequence, Eastern Christendom that was, for the most part, the home of theological learning. It was in Alexandria, Antioch and Syria that nearly all the heresies arose and it was in Councils held at Constantinople or its neighbouring cities, under the presidency of the Emperor, that they had been settled. In these Councils the Bishops of the West were a minority,

We must have very clearly in mind one important result of the heresy disputes of the fourth to the seventh centuries, for it had a profound effect upon the life of the Byzantine Empire and on the subsequent spiritual evolution of Christendom. The main subject of dispute in the Church in those centuries was the attempt to explain the two-fold nature of Christ, as both human and divine. The dispute was divided between three points of view, that of the Nestorians—so-called after their founder, Nestorius—who so emphasised the humanity of Christ as to accord Him two wholly separate natures; the Monophysites, who so exalted Christ's divine nature as completely to absorb His human nature into His divinity; and the Orthodox point of view which insisted on the presence of both natures in their fullness, united in Christ in one person.

The imperial demand for religious uniformity persecuted with varying rigour the two heretical Churches. The Nestorians were driven in to Persia, where at Nisibis and Jundi-Shapur they became a centre of Aristotelian philosophy and theological learning. The Monophysites of Antioch and Alexandria enjoyed occasional spells of imperial toleration, but, for the most part, preserved a precarious existence in the deserts of Egypt and Syria.

With the rise of the Saracen Empire, early in the seventh century, both these Churches passed under Arab rule, where they enjoyed a freedom of thought and worship which the Church of Constantinople had never tolerated. Under this tolerant Islamic rule the Monophysite Church spread, and in its monasteries there developed a deeper and less secular wisdom than that of the Nestorians, which tended to ally itself with Arabism. This Monophysite wisdom was to be the counter to the spiritual rigidity, both of Byzantine imperialism and later, of Roman papacy.

*　　*　　*

These facts give the general background of the events of 869 A.D., but we must bring the picture into closer focus. The Council of Constantinople of 869 A.D. was the aftermath of a century of the domination of Constantinople by a new heresy, one less of belief than of practice. The seventh century had ended in a welter of political confusion and intrigue. Moreover, it was not only the state which was corrupt but also the Church. While Constantinople was a city of intense religious observance, it was not itself a centre of religious learning. Its monastic orders did not give themselves to study, like those of the Nestorian and Monophysite Churches. The spiritual and philosophical interpretation of Christianity of the first three centuries, as it had found expression in Clement and Origen, had been abolished by Justinian in the sixth century, and had been replaced by a cult of the Liturgy, intensified by pilgrimages to holy places, especially those of Palestine. But the Saracen Conquest of Syria and Palestine had closed Jerusalem to Constantinople. In place of the sacred pilgrimages there had grown up a veneration of images and relics, and this developed into superstition and charlatanry among both monks and people. The better-educated classes and the leading hierarchy were opposed to these practices, but they made little headway against them.

In 717 A.D. a distinguished general, Leo the Isaurian, seized the imperial throne. He came from the mountainous country of Isauria in southern Asia Minor, a land of hardy warriors, that had known the spiritually intellectual impact of the Monophysite Church and, for a century the neighbourhood of Islam, both of them opposed to the use of images in worship. With his reform of the army and the civil administration, Leo also ordered the immediate removal of all images from the city and its churches. There was a popular outcry and violent opposition from the monks, but the Emperor retaliated with persecution and banishment, and the suppression of many monasteries. The situation was parallel to the Puritan and Catholic strife in England in the 16th and 17th centuries. Leo was supported by the better-educated classes and many of the more learned hierarchy.

Another result of the rise of the new dynasty, and one of the greatest consequence, was the gradual flow-back from the East of Aristotelian learning, and a revival in Constantinople itself of the Greek culture which Justinian had banished from the Empire two centuries before.

This iconoclastic tyranny, with varying rigour or leniency, continued for 60 years till 779 A.D., when the dowager Empress Irene, herself an "image-worshipper," [6] seized the power from her young son and reversed

---

[6] "Image-worshippers" ("iconodouloi") was the name given by the iconoclasts (image-destroyers) to those who used images in worship. The latter declared that the accusation was false, and that they only *venerated* images and relics because of their sacred associations. While this

Imperial policy. The violence of the iconoclasts had outrun their first reforming zeal, and amounted to opposition not only to the veneration of images, but to all external expressions of piety and even to monasticism itself. Moreover, in their persecution they had ruthlessly destroyed works of art and had banished Byzantine artists. All this had provoked a reaction which allied itself with the recovery of Greek culture and created amongst the moderates of both parties a desire for "economia," a policy of freedom of conscience. The Empress did not commit the city to monastic reaction. She restored the worship of images, but she had appointed as Patriarch, Tarasius, a layman and a moderate, who was President of the Imperial Chancellery.

There immediately followed an event of the greatest importance. A Synod of the whole Church was called at Nicaea in 787 A.D., at which iconoclasm was declared a heresy and, at the same time, the permissible use of images in worship was defined. This Synod is of importance to our present study because reference to it occurs frequently in the conflict between Rome and Constantinople that raged round the Council of 869 A.D. But it has an even greater importance for the spiritual understanding of the Council, yet one to which I have found no reference by any historian. The second canon of the Synod of Nicaea in 787 A.D. laid upon all bishops and clergy the essential duty of deep and constant study of the scriptures, and concluded with these words. "For the essence of our hierarchy is the divinely transmitted oracles, that is, the true knowledge of the Holy Scriptures, as the great Dionysius has declared it; and should anyone doubt this and not find his pleasure in thus acting and teaching, let him not be ordained."

How did it come to pass that this official acknowledgement of the authority of Dionysius' teaching is found in a Council of the whole Church, to which the Pope of that time set his seal, only 80 years before the Council of Constantinople of 869 A.D. abolished the Dionysian belief in the threefold nature of man as body, soul and spirit? How had this teaching established itself at orthodox Constantinople, where it had been rejected two centuries earlier, in the condemnation of Origen?

*　　　*　　　*

Every student of Anthroposophy knows how often and with what emphasis Rudolf Steiner spoke of the mysterious figure, Dionysius the Areopagite, who retained and taught the ancient Mystery teaching about

---

was for the most part true, the iconoclastic mind drew no distinction between veneration and worship.

the spiritual being of man in the light of Christianity, which teaching, though banned by the Roman Church, continued in subterranean currents, bursting up again and again in the mystic life of European Christendom. The writings of Dionysius appeared in Greek in the last 20 years of the fifth century in Egypt. They were deeply coloured with Neo-Platonism, and were associated with a revival in Egypt at that time of the teaching of Origen. The fact that the claim that the author of the writings was the New Testament Dionysius the Areopagite has been rejected by scholars is of little importance. It was quite traditional to publish writings under a famous name of the past, and in any case occult teaching was preserved in secret oral tradition long before it was made public. The important fact is the great part which these writings played in the subsequent history of the Church, in the west as well as in the east. Evelyn Underhill[7] considered that the influence of Augustine on the history of mysticism was as nothing compared with that of Dionysius the Areopagite. Nevertheless, how did this teaching win such authoritative approval at the Council of Nicaea in 787 A.D.?

A clue to this problem is to be found in the fact that there was also a Syriac source of teaching, as early as and possibly earlier than the Greek text. This affords us a definite and most important link with its appearance at Constantinople in the eighth century.

We have already spoken of the scholarly Monophysite monasteries. One of the most famous of these was set up in the fifth century at Edessa in northern Syria, from which the Nestorians had lately fled before the Catholic persecution. In the late part of the century a Monophysite monk of Edessa, Stephen bar Sudhaili, made a pilgrimage to Egypt where, we are told, he met Monophysite monks who had secretly revived the teaching of Origen. Stephen returned to Edessa and produced a work in Syriac on these lines. Thus the writings appeared, both in Greek and Syriac, at the end of the fifth century, through the activity of the Monophysite Church, and continued to be much used by the Monophysites.

The next link in our research is the fact that the Monophysite monastery of Edessa, while not an academy, had become a centre of learning as distinguished as the Persian University at Jundi-Shapur or that of the Nestorians at Nisibis, and was specially famous in the seventh

---

[7]   Evelyn Underhill was a well-known Authur of books on Mysticism in the nineteen twenties and thirties; she held a number of academic posts on religion at Oxford, Manchester and London.

century for the teaching of Greek  Here we have a direct connection with the influx of Greek culture into Constantinople with the coming of the Isaurian dynasty in 717 A.D.  With this Christian Greek culture would come the knowledge of the Dionysian teaching, acting as a counter to the merely worldly learning of the more violent iconoclasts, and to the superstition of the more fanatical image-worshipers.

Meanwhile the leniency of the Synod of Nicaea towards the recanting iconoclastic bishops and priests aroused the resentment of the fanatical image-worshipping monks, and, relying on the support of the Empress, they gave way to violence and disorder.  The result was that when Irene was supplanted by one of the State officials, she and her extremist party were so unpopular that imperial iconoclastic persecution broke out afresh and continued, with the exception of two short periods, until 843 A.D.

One of these periods adds another item to our knowledge of the Dionysian stream, and a most interesting one.  In 820 A.D. Michael the Stammerer, a native of Phrygia, came to the throne, and he instantly ordered complete freedom of thought for all his subjects.  During his short reign of nine years a Frankish Embassy came to Constantinople, seeking the imperial approval of the Pope's appointment of Louis the Pious, king of the Franks, as Emperor of the West.  Together with his consent Michael sent to Louis a Greek copy of the works of Dionysius.  It is significant that a teacher in the Schools of Paris at that time was the Irish monk, Scotus Erigena, whose subsequent translation of Dionysius into Latin deeply influenced the later mysticism of Western Christianity.

At last in 843 A.D., the Dowager Empress Theodora, like the former Empress Irene, an "image-worshipper," succeeded to the regency during the minority of her infant son, and immediately the images were restored. From this time the issue was no longer between iconoclasts and "image-worshippers," but between the extremist party who desired the suppression of the former iconoclasts and the moderate party who sought unity and peace.  Theodora herself realised that the policy of "economia" was now a necessity, and she appointed to the patriarchate Methodius, a bishop of the moderate party, and to the imperial chancellery Photius, the nephew of Tarasius.  Immediately the extremist monks , opposed alike to learning and freedom of conscience, broke out into insurrection and violence.  In 847 A.D. Methodius died, and Theodora, anxious to offend neither party, appointed as Patriarch a pious, but unfanatical, monk named Ignatius.  It was from this point that the events took place that led up to the Council of 869 A.D.

In 856 A.D. the young Emperor, Michael III, came of age, a pleasure-loving, but able, ruler who had little sympathy with monkish extremism. He moved away from his mother's control and associated himself with his uncle Bardas, who had been co-regent with Theodora. A plot was laid against Bardas and Ignatius allowed himself to be involved in it. The insurrection was suppressed, Theodora was immured in a convent, and Ignatius was arrested and banished. To save deprivation, and almost certainly under some constraint, Ignatius resigned the patriarchate. In appointing his successor the young emperor determined to avoid the conflict between the moderates and the extremists by disregarding the bishops of both parties. He turned to a layman, Photius, the President of the Imperial Chancellery. Within a week Photius had been ordained deacon and priest, consecrated as bishop, and installed as Patriarch. There was precedent for this. It had happened to his uncle Tarasius and to Nicephorus, both of whom had also been President of the Imperial Chancellery.

Now Photius is one of the two protagonists in this great conflict of the spirit, and we must pause to consider his personality. In the Western Church he has been constantly maligned as the author of the great schism between the East and the West. He was depicted as the bastard child of an escaped nun by a soldier of the Imperial Guard, and all kinds of defamatory legends were attached to him. In Eastern Christendom, on the other hand, he has always been lauded as a great saint and the champion of the Orthodox Church. A recent brilliant historical survey by Francis Dvornik justifies the Eastern viewpoint.

Photius belonged, in fact, to one of the great families of Constantinople. He was a Greek and not an iconoclast. Both he and his father had been persecuted as "image-worshippers." But above everything else he was one of the most famous scholars of the Middle Ages, and was regarded by post-Renaissance philosophers and philologists as the one most responsible for making available to Western Europe the knowledge of Greek and Hellenistic culture. He was spoken of by the Emperor Michael as "a man of colossal industry and almost universal knowledge, which he had received from no masters." This reputation, together with his name Photius, the Enlightened One, would seem to point in him to the intuitive knowledge of the Initiate. In him the Dionysian teaching, which his uncle Tarasius had embodied in the canons of the Synod of Nicaea, had reached a still higher level of expression. A man of high moral rectitude and spiritual insight, his own letters reveal how deeply he felt the wrench of leaving the calm fields of university scholarship and mystical meditation for the notoriously turbulent arena of religious party strife, for which, he declared, he felt the utmost contempt. Having, however, once accepted the patriarchate, he became the indomitable champion of the domestic independence of the Patriarchate of Constantinople against the growing claims of the papal primacy and its political plotting against the Byzantine Empire.

This Roman policy was especially embodied in Pope Nicholas I, who was the counter-protagonist to Photius in this conflict, and before we resume the course of events we must consider also the personality of Nicholas. Although he was Pope for only nine years, from 858 to 867 A.D., he was the leading figure in events which had a permanent effect on the history of Christendom, both in the west and in the east. Rudolf Steiner spoke of him as a great figure faced by difficult decisions at a critical moment. Since the division of the Empire in the fourth century, the influence of the Pope of Rome had gradually increased. Successive waves of barbarian conquest from the north had restricted the authority of the Byzantine Emperor in Italy almost to the exarchy of Ravenna. But most of the invaders were nominally Christian and venerated the person of the Pope, who, especially in the case of strong men like Gregory I, came to wield, not only spiritual, but also secular power, and felt themselves to be the focal point of the Western Empire. In 801 A.D. Leo III had consecrated Charlemagne as Emperor of the West, and when, after his death, the Frankish Kingdom began to break up, the Pope came to hold the position of king-maker. This, together with the traditional spiritual primacy of Rome, gave the Pope an independence of the authority of the Byzantine Emperor such as no other Christian patriarch possessed, and also set up a rivalry with the patriarchate of Constantinople that sowed the seed of an inevitable split between Eastern and Western Christendom.

This position had just matured when Nicholas, a man of great ability and spiritual perspicacity, came to the papal throne. He was immediately confronted with two decisions. In the first place the kingdom of Bulgaria, on the north side of the Adriatic, had recently been converted to Christianity by Frankish missionaries, and Nicholas saw it as an invaluable addition to the Roman Patriarchate, and a check to the western influence of Constantinople. On the other hand it was contiguous with the Byzantine frontier, and the Emperor regarded its possession and inclusion in the patriarchate of Constantinople as an invaluable protection against the growing thrust of the invading north. This political issue played a great part in the conflict between East and West that centred on the Council of 869 A.D.

But a deeper problem confronted Nicholas, a purely spiritual issue that was not manifest in surface events. It escapes the notice of most historians, although it found central expression in the Council of Constantinople. Rudolf Steiner explained it in detail.[8] Nicholas was concerned, not only with the political unity of the West, but with the spiritual unity of Western Christendom. He was aware of three spiritual streams that were spreading westward from the East, under the pressure of the Islamic conquest. The first stream was the mystical interpretation of Christianity that had developed in the first three centuries of Christendom among those who still possessed some of the occult perception that flowed from ancient Mystery knowledge, and which had ripened again in Neo-Platonism. It had found expression in Clement and Origen, and although, through Justinian, the Church had officially condemned it in the sixth century, it still survived among the Monophysites and was already raising its head in the Eastern Church under the name of Dionysius the Areopagite. Nicholas could not but be aware of the significance of the second canon of the Council of Nicaea in 787 A.D.

The second stream was a cult of spiritual Imagination, originating in Persia, which had spread along North Africa and was penetrating the West through Spain. It was the cult centred round the Mystery of the Graal.

The third stream was one which had developed in Constantinople, after the gradual disappearance of the stream of direct spiritual apprehension. It was a cult of the Liturgy, which provided worshippers with a direct experience of spiritual exaltation and a consciousness of supersensible reality.

These three streams were contrary to the spirit of Roman Christianity. Ever since the fourth century Rome had tended to express Christianity along the lines of traditional Roman thinking. The Roman conception of man as essentially a political unit in the Empire militated against the ancient conception of him as a spirit-being, which lay at the heart of the Greek ideal of liberty. The Papacy saw itself as the spiritual

---

[8] See *Building Stones for the Understanding of the Mystery of Golgotha; and Supersensible Influences in the History of Mankind.*

transformation of the Roman Empire, and conceived of Christendom as a spiritual empire held together by a legal system of dogma, in which the part of the individual was only that of unquestioning faith and absolute obedience. Any direct individual spirit-perception was suspect, and any organisation based on such a viewpoint must be suppressed as a heresy. Ever since the fourth century this spiritual policy had been organised in Italy and there stood behind Nicholas, and also behind his predecessor and successor, the figure of Anastasius the Librarian, a man of profound intellect and spiritual knowledge, who had made for himself a Latin translation of the works of Dionysius.

For all this Nicholas is not to be blamed. He was a man of great ability and far-seeing insight into what he conceived as the spiritual needs of Western Christendom. Rudolf Steiner emphasises this and speaks of "the necessity of Europeanised Christianity setting aside, from the concept of man, the idea of the spirit." It was the path that would lead to the evolution of European ego-consciousness, that has been the basis of western civilisation. But it must not be regarded as its ultimate goal.

Thus through a series of political and ecclesiastical circumstances, the spiritual issue was joined between Nicholas, the Pope of Rome, and Photius, the Initiate Patriarch of Constantinople.

*　　*　　*

To resume the narrative of events, in 857 A.D. Ignatius fell and Photius was appointed Patriarch. A Synod was held in Constantinople confirming this. In 859 A.D. Ignatius appealed to Pope Nicholas against his deposition and against Photius' uncanonical appointment. In 860 A.D. the Emperor Michael invited Nicholas to send legates to attend the General Council,[9] which he was summoning for a final elucidation of the Catholic doctrine about images. Nicholas consented on condition that his legates should at the same time examine the issue between Ignatius and Photius and report to him for his final decision. When the legates presented their letters, the Emperor objected that the issue between Ignatius and Photius was a domestic concern of Constantinople which was already settled, but as a concession, he consented to a re-trial of

---

[9] A *Synod* was a gathering of bishops, summoned and presided over by a patriarch.

A *General Council* was a gathering of bishops, summoned and presided over by the Emperor. In the West the decline of imperial authority transferred this power to the Pope. Although Nicholas claimed this power as of right, his successor called upon the Emperor to summon the General Council of 869.

An *Œcumenical Council* is a status given to a previous Synod or General Council by the subsequent General Council. The Canons of an œcumenical Council are binding upon the whole Church.

Ignatius by the legates, provided that they came to an immediate decision, without further reference to Rome. This was agreed. Ignatius was condemned and Photius' appointment was ratified, and the legates returned to Rome to report their decision to the Pope. For a while Nicholas took no action, except to send letters to the Emperor and to Photius demanding the return of the ancient province of Illyricum, which included Bulgaria. The dispute at Constantinople appeared to be an excellent opportunity for the exercise of power politics. But to his letters he received no reply.

Meanwhile, in 863 A.D., the representatives of the extremist party in Constantinople arrived in Rome, asking for a re-trial of Ignatius and secretly promising their support in the matter of Bulgaria. Immediately Nicholas summoned a Synod at Rome, rejected the decision of his legates, nullified Ignatius' deposition, and vilified and deposed Photius. Letters to this effect were sent to the Emperor and to Photius.

In 864 A.D. Michael conquered Bulgaria. The Bulgarian king was baptized and applied to Photius for a patriarch of his own. Photius replied that at present that was impossible. In 865 A.D. the Emperor sent a scathing reply to Nicholas, denying his right to interfere in the domestic affairs of the patriarchy of Constantinople, for which, as the New Rome, he claimed equal status with Old Rome. He made no reference to Bulgaria, but demanded the immediate return of the extremist Byzantines under threat of military action. This letter found Nicholas seriously ill, and the reply was drafted by Anastasius, in no less strong terms than Michael's letter. It made, for the first time, an explicit claim, not only to the primacy of Rome, but to its complete authority over the whole Church. It declared that the Pope alone had authority to summon a General Council—a complete disregard for all historical precedent. It also refused to send back the dissident Byzantines.

Suddenly an unexpected move by King Boris of Bulgaria gave a new turn to the crisis. In 866 A.D. he sent envoys to the Pope, making the same request which Photius had refused. Nicholas immediately dispatched two bishops to Bulgaria, with orders to expel the Greek priests. He also sent legates with further peremptory letters to Michael and Photius. When the legates arrived they were kept waiting six weeks at the port. Meanwhile, the expelled Greek priests arrived from Bulgaria and reported that the Romans were tolerating the heretical practices of the Frankish missionaries, the eating of milk and cheese in Lent, the enforcement of clerical celibacy, the restriction of the right to confirm to bishops only, and finally, the inclusion of the word "filioque"[10] in the Creed, contrary to the credal form authorised by the first Œcumenical Council of Nicaea 500 years previously.

Photius immediately called a Synod and then, in 867 A.D., a Council, which was attended, not only by the Eastern bishops, but by a number of Western bishops who were opposed to Nicholas. The Council passed canons, condemning the Frankish heresies, condemning Pope Nicholas and demanding his deposition, declaring Louis II Emperor of the West—a bid for lay support—and finally declaring the Synod of Nicaea of 787 A.D. to be the Seventh Œcumenical Council, and so binding on the whole Church.

This was the first occasion on which the "filioque" dispute, which caused the final split between Eastern and Western Churches, had been made an official issue, and for this reason Photius was always condemned by the West as the author of the schism. But Photius did not accuse Pope Nicholas of holding this heretical view, but only of tolerating its propagation by the Franks. The issue was not yet a theological one, but a question of credal orthodoxy. The Franks had claimed at the beginning of the eighth century that the "filioque" clause was part of the original Creed. The East replied that it was not in the Creed adopted in the First Œcumenical Council of Nicaea in 325 A.D. Pope Leo III agreed with this view and had the Nicene Creed engraved on silver plates and stored in Rome. Also the "libellus," or declaration of orthodoxy used at all Synods and Councils, contained the Creed in the Nicene form. It was not until the *eleventh* century that a German pope forced the Italians to insert into the Creed the "filioque" clause, and it was not discussed as a theological issue until the Council of Florence in 1439 A.D. The theological question about the nature of the Holy Spirit did not arise in this dispute, and is in any case a quite different issue to the denial by the Western Church of the threefold nature of man.

*     *     *

The Emperor and Photius were deeply angered by the papal letters and by the Roman intrigue with Bulgaria, and felt themselves to be in a very strong position. But the public condemnation of Nicholas was impetuous and ill-judged. Unknown to Photius, Nicholas had already died, and his successor Hadrian, no admirer of Nicholas, was hesitating

---

[10] Filioque meaning, and the Son—The question as to whether the Holy Spirit came from the Father and the Son or only from the Father.

as to what line he should take. A more conciliatory action might have won him over.

At that moment an unexpected act of political treachery wrecked Photius' position and entirely altered the course of events. Basil, a friend of Michael, having already secured, in the spring of 867 A.D., the assassination of Bardas, Michael's uncle, in the autumn murdered the young Emperor himself and seized the throne, probably encouraged in this by Rome and the extremist party. To secure his position, Basil immediately reversed the Imperial policy. He wrote to Pope Hadrian, accepting Nicholas' decision of 863, deposing Photius. Photius immediately resigned and Ignatius was restored. Basil's letter decided Hadrian and the arrival in Rome of the Acts of the Photian Council of 867 confirmed his resolution. He immediately summoned a Synod in Rome, and condemned Photius to deprivation and excommunication without hearing his defence. The canons of the Council of 867 A.D. were revoked and its Acts publicly burned. The primacy and supreme authority of the Pope were confirmed.

Immediately a demand was sent to Basil to summon a General Council, which was to meet under the presidency of the papal legates, in order to ratify and carry out the Pope's sentence. The Emperor was in no position to refuse and the Council met in Constantinople in 869 A.D. But Basil in his own capital was not in the same mood as the suppliant to Rome. He insisted on presiding in the person of his own representative, Baanes, and, to the indignation of the legates, he also insisted on their presenting their credentials and signing the usual declaration of orthodoxy. Moreover, he decreed that Photius must be heard in his own defence.

The legates took a very arrogant line, that there was nothing for the Council to debate. All that was to be done was to confirm the resolutions passed at Rome. The Byzantines were humiliated, with the exception of Photius himself, who, with true Initiate understanding of the rigged situation, refused to utter a word in his own defence, except that, at one point, he urged the legates to do penance! Finally, on the proposal of the legates, Photius was excommunicated.

Among the canons of the Council was the one to which Rudolf Steiner specifically refers as banishing the spirit from the constitution of man. It must be remembered that the wording of this canon presented an entirely Roman point of view, for all the canons had been drawn up by Anastasius at Rome and passed at the Roman Synod, and were only mechanically confirmed by the Council at Constantinople. This canon is hardly noticed by commentators. Dvornik does not mention it in his actual account of the Council, but only refers to it in another context as an instance of a fabricated charge against Photius. "Photius," he declares, "could not have been guilty of so crude a heretical utterance."

It is clear that Dvornik does not relate the canon to the demand for the œcumenicity of the Council of 787 A.D., with its recognition of the authority of Dionysius the Areopagite. It is in this light, however, that the reference to "two souls" is comprehensible. In point of fact, the charges in the canon are set out at considerable length, and its fierce denunciatory tone and detailed anathemas show that Anastasius was aware here of the deep spiritual issue between Rome and Constantinople of which Rudolf Steiner speaks.

The following is a literal translation of the canon.

*"Although the Old and New Testaments both teach that man has one rational and intellectual soul, and all the divinely-inspired Fathers and teachers of the Church express the same opinion, certain men, given over to the pursuit of evil, have reached such a pitch of impiety as to enunciate the dogma that a man has two souls, and, by a certain irrational exploitation of a wisdom, which has already been made folly,[11] seek to establish this heresy. Therefore this holy and Catholic Synod, hastening to root out, like utterly evil tares, this worthless belief, holding in its right hand the winnowing fan of truth, that it may cast out this chaff to the unquenchable flame, and present the world as the field of Christ, anathamatizes with a loud voice the inventors and perpetrators of such an impiety, together with those who share their views, and decrees that no one shall pay any regard or obedience to the decrees of the author of this impiety.[12] And if anyone dares to act contrary to the decrees of this holy and great Synod, let him be anathema, and an outcast from the faith and fellowship of Christians."*

To those who are aware of the Dionysian background, the reference here to man possessing two souls is clear. The Dionysian teaching was linked up with Origenism and Neo-Platonism, and, through that, Neo-Pythagoreanism. Pythagoras (555 B.C.) had had direct access to Mystery knowledge and he taught that the being of man has three parts: "Nous" (Thinking), "Thumos" (Feeling and Desire), and "Phrenes" (Bodily

---

[11] The denunciation of Origenism in 555.
[12] A clear reference to Photius.

Instinct). "Nous" is the sphere of the activity of spirit, "Thumos" that of the soul, "Phrenes" that of the body. Of these the first only is sinless and immortal. By the ordinary man this is naturally understood as saying that "man has two souls, one of which is sinless." This would be anathema to the Roman conception of man as totally corrupt. In the thirteenth century the Scholastics justified their holding of "the double truth" on the ground that man's thinking had shared in the consequence of the Fall. This Thomas Aquinas could not accept, although at that very time it was in the process of becoming true!

We must note carefully the words in the canon, "man has one rational and intellectual soul." Steiner tells us that previously the phrase had been "one imaginative and spiritual soul," thus avoiding any separate mention of spirit. In the words of the canon there is a deliberate denial that man's " thinking and rational" faculty is anything more than a *soul* quality, and there is a deliberate *exclusion of spirit.*

          *            *

The defeat of Photius did not last long. In 870 A.D. Hadrian died and was succeeded as Pope by John VIII. In 873 A.D. Photius was recalled from banishment and restored to communion, and in 876 A.D. was reconciled to Ignatius. In 877 A.D. Ignatius died and immediately the clergy of Constantinople elected Photius as Patriarch, and this was finally accepted by the Pope as a *fait accompli.* In 879 A.D. Basil summoned a General Council to ratify the existing situation in Constantinople and to rehabilitate Photius, and asked the Pope to send legates. The Emperor, owing to his own absence on account of the sudden death of his son, appointed Photius himself to preside. All anti-Photian Synods were suppressed, the Acts of the Council of 869 A.D. were reversed, and, finally, the Council of Nicaea of 787 A.D. was declared once more to be the Seventh Œcumenical Council, under threat of excommunication of all who dissented. The resolutions embodying the Council's decisions were actually proposed by one of the papal legates, and were carried unanimously.

For the moment the conflict was at an end, but the seed had been sown which could only result in the ultimate division between Eastern and Western Christendom. From that time their paths diverged.

In the West the Council of Nicaea of 787 A.D. was not accepted as Œcumenical for some centuries. Meanwhile there was established under absolute papal authority a body of clearly defined dogma and ritual, to be accepted unquestionably by faith alone. Moreover, the Western Church adhered to the decision of the Council of 869 A.D. in regard to the twofold being of man, as soul and body. Aristotelian in origin, it fitted into the Roman framework of Grammar and Rhetoric in which the clergy expressed their theological concepts, and also into the evolving individual self-consciousness of man, in which his thinking appeared to him to arise out of himself. Through its exposition by Scotus Erigena the teaching of Dionysius spread into monastic studies, but it centred most entirely upon the understanding of the Being of God. It had no effect on the official western concept of the being of man.

Meanwhile among the early Scholastics there awoke the query as to the real nature and the reliability of man-derived concepts, a doubt fanned by the invading pantheism of Arabism. It began to penetrate even into the sacred realm of dogma. For a while Thomas Aquinas stemmed the rising tide of doubt by drawing from sources of earlier wisdom an understanding of the deeper activities of thought within man himself. Thereby he reconciled philosophy and theology up to the point beyond which, he said, human reason had no authority. But within a generation the doubt returned, to be gradually strengthened by scientific discovery into a sole reliance upon human sense-derived thinking, which has to a great extent captured many fields of religious thought.

But the deeper Dionysian teaching of the pathway to direct spirit knowledge by-passed the orthodox rigidity of Rome. It reached the West through the now independent patriarchate of Bulgaria, and during the deepening doubt from the thirteenth to the sixteenth centuries, it inspired a succession of mystical thinkers in South Germany and England.

For Eastern Christendom, on the other hand, the triumph of Photius was the beginning of an era of learning and spiritual culture in the Church of Constantinople, that lasted for over 500 years. The use of images in worship which had been restored was strictly controlled under ecclesiastical regulations. No three-dimensional image was allowed in any Orthodox church, but only the two-dimensional icon, or else mosaic. Strict rules also governed the painting of icons, which were Imaginations, rather than the physical representations found in Western sacred art. They expressed and evoked the spirit behind the physical. They were the meeting in art of the "two paths" of Dionysius; the Greek representation of the physical and the Monophysite apprehension of the spiritual.

Perhaps the contrast between the Western and Eastern Churches is most clearly seen in the comparison of their Eucharistic worship. The Western Mass became a doctrinally-defined, hierarchically enacted, divine miracle, which the worshippers, convinced of their inherent sinfulness, partook of or beheld in hope of forgiveness and future immortality. The Eastern Liturgy was an undefined rite of Initiation, in which each worshipper participated, and experienced anew each time the transformation and renewal of being as spirit. The earthly man became the receptacle of the suprasensible reality and was transformed into the heavenly man. The Dionysian vision of the threefold being of man has always remained as the essence of the mystical thinking and teaching of the Orthodox Church. The long subjugation of the Orthodox Church to Turkish rule kept its outlook from being influenced by Western evolution.

To-day the greatest need of mankind is the recovery of the knowledge of man's true eternal self as spirit, and that knowledge must develop above all in the Christian Church itself. It was with surprise and delight that recently I heard an Oxford theologian say in a Convocation debate, "Theologians are beginning to turn away from the Western idea of twofold man, back to the Eastern idea of man as spirit, soul and body."

# CHRIST AND THE MODERN MAN[13]

I CONSIDER it a great compliment to have been asked to give this second Maurice Elliott Memorial lecture. I met the Rev. Maurice Elliott only on a few occasions, but I was always impressed by his simplicity and sincerity. I have been deeply moved by the account of his life which Miss White very kindly sent to me. He was a real Christian martyr and faithful witness, accepting the deprivations and rebuffs which ecclesiastical authority inflicted on him without moving one inch from his convictions and, which is far rarer, without one trace of rancour. The immovability of his convictions was no doubt due to his own psychic gifts, and especially to the developed clairvoyance of his wife, which led them to direct supersensible experiences which left no room for doubt. It was providential that he was available as one of the founders and for so long the Secretary of the Churches' Fellowship for Psychical Study. Its formidable list of Episcopal patrons to-day shows how the Church's official attitude towards psychical investigation has changed since Maurice Elliott was first associated with the Society.

My own interest in psychic phenomena goes back fifty years, but for the past twenty years it has been concentrated upon the Spiritual Science—or Anthroposophy, as it is also called—of Rudolf Steiner. Spiritual Science has in the deepest sense the same aim as that of the C.F.P.S., viz. the study and knowledge of spiritual realities and their relation to our physical life and experience. But Steiner's approach to this problem differed from that of most people. Owing to his lifelong clairvoyance, his awareness was not that of psychic phenomena breaking in unexpectedly upon an established physical consciousness and demanding verification and explanation, but of two equally clear and self-consistent levels of perception from childhood, revealing two different sets of phenomena, sometimes separate, sometimes interwoven. This situation provoked a constant urge in him to discover the relation between these two worlds of experience, more particularly because to all his acquaintance there was only one world, that of sense experience, which was to be explained only in terms of that experience.

As he arrived at the threshold of manhood Steiner discovered the relation between his two worlds, and that the bridge between them was thought-controlled meditation upon the phenomena of the physical world.

---

13  The Second Maurice Elliott Memorial Lecture 30/11/1961.

Each level of consciousness was also a manifestation of a new level of being, and he discovered that in man there were four levels of being and consciousness. In fact man is a *spiritual-physical* being, in whom four levels of being and consciousness are interwoven, although he is only conscious at the lowest, the physical level.

Moreover, he perceived that these levels of being were to be found, in varying degree, in the universe about him. It was really a self-discovery, which provided a pathway from the spiritual in man to the spiritual in the universe. It launched Steiner on a lifelong endeavour to bring to man—then entering the phase of scientific materialism—the conviction of the fact of spirit reality in himself and in the universe, not as succeeding to or alongside of physical existence, but as interwoven with it at different levels of consciousness, as its origin, its source and its sustenance. He also strove to make plain the path along which such discovery can be made.

Now beyond the attempt to establish the reality of the spiritual or supersensible, there is a special element in the study of psychic phenomena that is of deep importance to all Christians, as it was to Maurice Elliott, and as it is to the C.F.P.S. It is the relation of all this to the Christian faith, to the historical fact of the Incarnation, and to the living Christ. To Christian enquirers it is the relation of a new discovery to an accepted faith and a known experience. As we shall see, this element in the spiritual understanding of man and the universe became of fundamental importance also to Rudolf Steiner, but he arrived at it in quite another way. He had not been brought up in the Christian faith and his scientifically-trained mind felt a natural antipathy to the Church's defence of its point of view by an appeal to dogma and authority. It was not, therefore, in seeking to reconcile his views with accepted convictions and beliefs, but in a new and—as it was to St. Paul—an unexpected and overwhelming vision of the event of Calvary, that Steiner came to the discovery of the relationship of Christ and His Incarnation to the spiritual-physical world he had come to understand. It became central to his whole outlook. He came to see Christ as the Alpha and Omega of spirit and matter, the author and goal of the being of man and the universe, his Incarnation the central fact of human history, interpreting man's past, making possible man's true future, and he saw the right earthly relationship to Christ as the most vital need of every human being. It was another pathway to Christ to that of orthodox Christianity.

Now it is because of this vital need of man to discover the significance of Christ in his world outlook that I chose for the title of this lecture, "Christ and the modern man". For it is the claim of the Christian Church that in, and only in, his relation to Christ and His deed for mankind can each individual find eternal salvation. Yet to-day modern man is for the most part unaware of Christ. He sees neither the vision, nor its relevance to himself and his world. Nor is this strange. For twentieth century man is another being to that which he was almost up to the nineteenth century, living in another world, which contains elements that seem irreconcilable with the traditional Christ-presentation.

For example, up to the nineteenth century man lived on the known material earth, its phenomena were related to him in different ways as external objects, and the heavens were the manifestation of a surrounding spiritual world. To-day he looks out on a vast and, apparently, ever-expanding universe, in which spatially the earth seems utterly unimportant. It is strange and new, by its vastness, by the sudden insecurity of the existence of the earth itself, and by the assumption of the possibility of the extension of man's experience in his self-centred, rational body, out into the universe. How can a long past incident on this tiny planet have any relevance to so vast a picture?

Again, until the nineteenth century man lived as an individual in his visible, sense-controlled body, happy or unhappy, idealistic and wayward, good and evil, a simple comprehensible existence, at the end of which, for the most part, he cherished the Christian hope of immortality. To-day there has arisen, from the hitherto unperceived depths of his being, the Unconscious, not only as a revelation but more and more as an experience. It yawns before him, dark, threatening, engulfing, shedding bewilderment on his origin, his destiny, his free-will, even on any hope of a possible individual future; excusing, yet riveting his failures upon him. To-day more and more people are like souls locked in the prison of their own Unconscious. What can the message of deliverance and immortality after death mean to those unable to escape from this earthly prison?

Or again, to turn to history. At the beginning of the nineteenth century history was bounded by Homer or Abraham. To-day man is taught to see it as an age-long evolution from the lowest animal form, and in human history itself involving vast periods of the history of other races and peoples, great civilisations, that rose and fell centuries before Christ, others since then who never knew Him, and others to-day, indifferent and seemingly independent of Him. In the nineteenth century man was but

86

dimly and impersonally aware of other races, even of other nations, than his own. To-day men of all creeds and colour are mingled together, their consciousness is becoming increasingly unified, and more and more are they all being caught up in this twentieth century bewilderment. How can this two thousand years old story of a Christ, for a few brief years incarnate in a Galilean peasant-prophet, a story evolved through western culture into the pattern of the Christian Churches of to-day, be made relevant and convincing to this manifold world of humanity? How can the traditional presentation of Christianity be adequate to such a task? What can Christ mean to the modern man?

Of course, to the convinced Christian the gospel of Christ is still a way of personal salvation and power, carrying with it a belief in its ultimate victory in the world. But this belief is often held alongside and in defiance of the stupendous and terrifying background of the present world situation. It does not attempt to include its problems nor to answer the bewildering questions they raise. The Christian for the most part side-steps the issue in faith and in a resigned agnosticism as to the answers. But how can the modern man who has not this background of faith—exalted, bewildered, stupefied, frightened, frustrated, or just living as best he can from day to day—how can he find Christ out of such a world-experience?

There are three recognised paths to the discovery of Christ. The first is the historical accounts in the four Gospels, the second is the Christian tradition and life manifest in the Christian Churches, and the third is the direct individual experience of the Christ, what we may call Christian conversion. This last is an incommunicable path, and we have already seen that the first two do not appear in the eyes of modern man to be adequate to the drastically altered background of human life and experience. A fourth path has been opened up in the last hundred years, and in the last forty years it has become a more clearly defined and recognisable path. This is the study of psychic or spiritual phenomena, with which this Society is so directly and effectively concerned. One of its chief results has been to lead men and women back to the two recognised paths of the Bible and the Churches, by confirming by direct evidence many elements in their presentation about which modern doubt had arisen. But I think it would be agreed that the evidence is chiefly in regard to spirit reality and human survival of death. There is not a coherent pattern in such psychic phenomena which will provide an answer to the new and perplexing phenomena in regard to man and the universe which confront and bewilder the modern man, or lead to a real discovery of the Christ which embraces these perplexities, and, in so doing, meets man's deepest spiritual needs both in this life and in that which lies beyond it.

Finally, there is the pathway to Christ which, as we have already related, Rudolf Steiner discovered for himself, and in which he found such certainty of understanding and such relevance to the modern picture of man and the universe that he gave his whole life to making it ever clearer, pointing his fellow-men to it as the path to which the spiritual world is calling mankind to-day, at this moment of its greatest physical and spiritual danger. In seeking to present to you this path, which Steiner opened up over many years, in many books and lectures, you will understand that I can only attempt to indicate the stages of its discovery and the comprehensiveness of the vision to which it led.

I have already described how his attempt to understand his inborn clairvoyance led to the discovery of thought-controlled meditation as the bridge between spirit and matter, and how by this means he passed from world discovery to self-discovery, in which he was able to arrive at four successive levels of consciousness in himself, that were also four levels of being. It was in his experience of these successive levels of his own being that Steiner came to the understanding of man and the universe. So transformed was consciousness at each level that he declared that no level could be described until it was reached and experienced, and that it could not be really understood until the level above it had been attained.

At the first level above physical consciousness Steiner became aware of the spirit-background of the physical life of man and the universe. Through and out of that element in himself he perceived there flowed the forces which fashioned and maintained the life of his body, just as in the world of nature they maintained the life of plant and animal. Spirit was manifest as the origin of matter. But more than that, Steiner found himself in a new time-consciousness, in which the whole of his life, past and present, was before him as a tableau, of which each part was equally available, not only to memory, but to experience. Moreover, he discovered running through this tableau of his life, and pre-existent to it, a guiding pattern of events and relationships, around which it had formed itself, without constant or fatalistic compulsion. It seemed to be an unconscious self-direction, though its origin as a pre-existent pattern was not yet clear to him.

At the second level of being consciousness was once more transformed. No longer is he in a world of matter-forming forces, but in a world of spirit beings, and the tableau of his life, that before had been a tableau of incidents and events, is now a chain of personal relationships that had been inherent in those events, and which he now realises as the true and abiding essence of his earthly existence. New values rise within him, in a field of consciousness in which the Moral Law, which is the law of personal relationships, is the only law of being. Wider and further extends that realm of spirit beings around him, and in their presence there arises within him self-judgement, the need of purgation, of atonement.

But he makes a further discovery. Running through the chain of human relationships into which his earthly life has been transformed, he finds a pre-existent pattern of moral qualities and specific personal relationships. Clearly it must be related to the controlling pattern he had discovered at the lower level. But whence was it derived? He realises that it was fashioned in his own pre-earthly spiritual existence, out of the fruits and failures of a previous earth life.

In this way, Steiner discovered in actual perception the significance of that process of reincarnation, in which more than half of mankind has always believed, and about which in recent years so much speculation has gathered in western minds. He saw it, not as an unwilling, desire-compelled descent, again and again, into a world of illusion and death, as the East sees it; nor as an intriguing succession of earth lives. He saw it as the whole process of man's spiritual evolution, a rhythm of being between spirit and matter, a process of descent from spirit to matter, and then in re-ascent, the purging and harvesting of the spiritual result of each earth life, for renewal and re-equipment in the spirit world for another descent. For that return, the human spirit is fitted, at the soul-level of its descent, with the karmic qualities and relationships arising out of the previous earth life, thus ensuring the continuity of spirit-personality from life to life, and making possible the progress of spiritual evolution. This is Karma. At the spiritual-physical formative level this soul-pattern is metamorphosed into a pattern of event and circumstance, which expresses itself, in physical existence, in successional events and relationships in space and time. This space and time-conditioned physical life, hedged in by forgetfulness of the spirit world, may seem the nadir of human existence, but it is the one sphere of being in which man can, in freedom, achieve his spiritual evolution.

There still remains a fourth level of being, the level of spirit existence in the world of pure spirit. Of this Steiner says much, but it cannot effectively be summed up in a few words, so I will not attempt to describe now that wonderful process of complete self-discovery and spiritual re-equipment. But at the threshold of that final transformation Steiner describes a great event. He becomes aware of the presence of the Christ as the Alpha and Omega of the whole universe of being, but also as the Champion and Saviour of human evolution. In that awareness was revealed to him the true meaning of the Incarnation and of the Mystery of Golgotha. Christ is not to be understood merely as the divine Son of God who descended into earth life at a particular period in world history, in order that He might provide, for those who would accept Him, a way of safety through an evil world to a blissful spiritual future. He is the Christ of human destiny, who, by the deeds of countless spirit beings, formed and fashioned the process and means of man's spiritual evolution; who has overshadowed and shepherded mankind through all its earthly pilgrimage, manifesting Himself in varying ways in the great religions of the world, at that level of spiritual consciousness at which, at that time, mankind stood. Finally, at the threshold of the era when, in absorption into physical consciousness, man would discover his self-hood, yet risk losing his understanding of the spiritual nature and origin of his being—as is happening to-day—Christ manifested Himself in that lowly level of physical being in which man could apprehend Him. Thereby He delivered man from the powers that held him imprisoned in his past failures, and released into the world a spiritual impulse that would ensure the achievement of human spiritual evolution.

Steiner described that discovery of Christ within the process of reincarnation in arresting words.

*"For those who will lift themselves from Inspiration to Intuition there opens up a spiritual world which contains the Mystery of Golgotha like the mighty consolation within the whole world's existence."*

The task you in the C.F.P.S. and others have undertaken, of finding a path to the certainty of spirit reality, must go beyond the investigating and testing of psychic phenomena by seeking to bring them within the sphere of sense-perceptible proof. We must seek, by the awakening of our own latent spirit faculties, to apprehend them in their own sphere of working, and so relate them into an organic pattern of spirit reality, that will explain our expanding universe and meet the new problems of our own being. Even though most men and women to-day will not be able to climb the heights of metamorphosed consciousness and being that Steiner describes, the path still lies open to them. We do not need to be able to work out or even follow the mathematical formulae that underlie atomic science, before we can comprehend and absorb the new world outlook which it brings before us. So too in spirit discovery. If we take into our unprejudiced thinking this picture of reincarnation as the process of human evolution, we shall find in it the answer to the problems of the new world situation.

We shall find the working of the Unconscious explained at the first level of spiritual-physical, or etheric, being. Its many manifestations of mental abnormality will be seen to be due to an increasing unselfconscious awareness of some etheric phenomena, without an understanding of the new conditions of consciousness and being that interpret them. It is a confusion of physical and etheric consciousness. This is a danger which Steiner declared forty years ago would meet man in his unconscious spiritual evolution in the second half of this century, unless he achieved awareness and understanding of spirit reality.

So too, the vast picture of the meaningless masses and movements of the nebulae resolves itself into a universe of spirit beings, in infinite creative relationships to one another and to man. The perplexity of history, with its procession of rising and falling civilisations, is seen as mankind's pilgrimage of spiritual descent and ascent, in which we all have taken part, and in which recurring individual reincarnation is the principle of unification and progress. So too, the apparent inadequacy of a single earth life, or its bondage to physical or moral or circumstantial deficiency, is given new hope and understanding in the realisation of the process of reincarnation.

Finally, there is the certainty that in all this man has never been alone. The Christ, whose earthly incarnation the Gospels declare to us, has always shepherded man's path of evolution, and since his descent into our earthly life He is always with us, to be found of those who seek Him.

This path which Rudolf Steiner has laid before us is not one of spiritual arrogance or human self-sufficiency. The Christ-experience, Steiner declared, is dependent upon two convictions; first, the conviction of the incapacity of man to attain to it by his own unaided powers; and secondly, the certainty of the resurrecting power of the spirit, which Christ has won for man. With this approach it is a pathway along which the modern man can find Christ again.

# ANTHROPOSOPHY AND THE CHRISTIAN CHURCHES[14]

Although it is sixty years since Rudolf Steiner first began to expound his world-picture of the fundamental reality of spirit as the primary creative force throughout the universe, his teaching has been almost unnoticed by the Christian Churches. In its early stages this was largely accounted for by the historical situation. The birth of Anthroposophy at the opening of the twentieth century was historically a surprising phenomenon. Science, in the first flush of its confident development of the Darwinian theory of evolution, was complacently asserting the sufficiency of matter and its functions to explain the whole universe, including man him-self. The first violent orthodox reaction against the Darwinian theory had died down, and public opinion was gradually accepting the scientific view-point as proved. On the continent, and especially in Germany, where Haeckel's version of Darwinism had swept the board, Protestant theologians were humanizing Christianity, extracting from it almost everything that was supernatural. In the Protestant Churches of England and America theology was at a low ebb, and there was a complacent indifference to the apparent contradiction between credal and scientific beliefs, in the confident expectation that the world was getting better and better every day.

It was amazing that at that moment of complacent materialism, a young Austrian scientist, under the impulse of his own highly-developed supersensible faculties and of an over-mastering experience of Christ, should begin to expound factually the spirit background of man and the universe, and the working of spirit from the very beginning of creation, through the whole evolutionary process, up to its continuous immediate activity in the kingdoms of nature and in man. Moreover, that he should place at the pivotal point of this cosmic evolutionary process the person and earthly life of Christ, and expound in their full supernatural significance the recorded incidents of his life that so many theologians were engaged in explaining away. The first of his series of lectures and publications was an exposition of the full significance of the redemptive deed of Christ in the spiritual world-setting, and this was shortly followed by a similar treatment of the four Gospels.

---

[14] First published in Journal for Anthroposophy New York, U.S.A. 1966.

In his deliberately undertaken life-work of expounding the reality of spirit and its universal working it was almost inevitable that Steiner was at first brought into close contact with the Theosophical Movement, for that was the only movement at that time that was consciously based on the immediate apprehension of spirit reality. From the commencement this association was somewhat strained, for the Theosophical Movement sought its inspiration in the ancient spirit-wisdom of the East, while Steiner revealed spirit-knowledge as a new possibility of the present age, through the metamorphosis of the powers of thought which were the main-spring of western scientific progress. Moreover, Steiner's unswerving assertion of the crowning finality of the deed of Christ was distasteful to the Theosophical viewpoint which saw all religions as equally a manifestation of divine truth. In a few years, the Theosophical leaders could no longer tolerate this deep division of approach within their Society, and Steiner carried on his task independently under the title of Anthroposophy or Spiritual Science.

This movement was almost entirely confined to the Continent, but there Steiner travelled from country to country and from place to place in an almost ceaseless round of lectures, given to ever-increasing audiences of those who were seekers after the spirit. His great appeal was that he spoke out of direct perception of supersensible reality, and also fully expounded the methods by which ordinary human consciousness might acquire that faculty. He had just completed the full exposition of the spirit-nature of man and the universe, when, like an unexpected clap of thunder out of blue skies, the first World War shattered the complacency of mankind.

After the war, Steiner proceeded to establish his teaching by applying its principles to all departments of human life and social activity, and in those years he visited England and made a deep impression upon some of its leading thinkers. The Churches, however, were still impervious to his message. Only the Church of Rome, with its invariable opposition to any spiritual revelation that had not its immediate source in its own authority, showed open hostility to Anthroposophy. The other Churches in Germany were still too busy trimming revelation to the accepted scientific pattern, while to the Churches of England and America it was unknown or, at best, a strange foreign "ism".

In 1925 Rudolf Steiner died, and his followers, stunned by the loss of his personality, took a considerable time to organise and make effective their propagation of his work. To-day, however, Anthroposophy is a world-wide Movement and has imposed itself deeply on many departments of human life. Nevertheless, to-day, over forty years after Steiner's death, it remains almost unknown to and unnoticed by the Christian Churches. If this seemed strange at the beginning of the century, it is all the more amazing now, when the Churches are facing crises and problems in all directions. At the dawn of the Russian revolution in 1917, Dr. Steiner foretold the cataclysmic changes which would follow it, especially after the middle of the century. One after another they have occurred, National-Socialism, race-persecution, a second World War, an ordered and defiant political materialism which captures whole peoples, a cold war which toys with the menace of world destruction, and, above all a Science, which no longer concerns itself chiefly with the natural relationships between Earth and Man, but has penetrated to a sub-human level, at which, with brain washing, human processing, and artificial insemination, it denies or would destroy the spiritual being of man.

There are some Church leaders who comfort themselves with the fact that there is an increase in Church attendance in the last decade. This is undeniable, especially in the U.S.A., and there is no doubt that the uncertainty of the world-situation is driving many to the assurance and comfort of a gospel of personal salvation. No-one would deny or belittle the value of this personal attitude to Christianity, but its real effectiveness for humanity is in the measure in which it penetrates the every-day concepts of life in the world. A leading American writer in a recent interview declared that although perhaps 75% of the American people attended some place of worship on Sunday, during their week-day life almost all of them accepted unquestioningly the materialistic scientific interpretation of man and the universe.

*There*, in the enormous prestige of a materialistic Science, dominating, absorbing, fascinating the human mind, and especially that of the rising generation, is the problem that confronts the Christian Churches. To Science, with its astounding advances and almost daily breath-taking discoveries and anticipated possibilities, the Christian Faith is irrelevant, a possible solace to the individual, but of no vital significance to the evolutionary past or future of humanity, and, still less, of the universe. Personal religion will lack force, if indeed it can survive, with this divided outlook. The answer to it, is not to bring religious faith more into line with scientific opinion, though that seems to be the objective of a certain type of theology. It is to see whether a deeper

94

consideration of the factual findings of scientific observation will lead to conclusions consistent with Christian belief. It would appear that it is the scientist himself, rather than the theologian, who doubts the certainty of scientific conclusions. Pierre Teilhard de Chardin is a Jesuit priest, but in *The Phenomenon of Man*, his penetrating criticism of scientific materialism, he writes as a scientist.

But more directly menacing to the Churches than the theoretical materialism of Science is the deliberate hostility of the powerfully organised social and political system of Communism, based upon a complete denial of spirit in man and the universe. Already it dominates two-fifths of the human race and it expands by ceaseless and ruthless propaganda. It can only be effectively countered by proving the reality of spirit and manifesting the nature of its working at every level of being.

Yet another problem that confronts world-Christianity is the rapidly increasing racial and national consciousness in the non-white peoples. It manifests itself in a deep antipathy to European and American domination. The Christian religion, which perforce has been propagated under the forms of its western historical evolution, is coming to be regarded as a foreign importation, and the revival of the indigenous religion as a symbol of independent self-development.

Finally, there is a problem that only came to the fore three years ago by the publication in 1963 of the Bishop of Woolwich's book, "Honest to God," which has received great publicity and a considerable measure of approval. This problem is all the more serious inasmuch as it has had its source within the Christian Churches themselves. It is an attempt to bridge the gulf between members of the Christian Churches and those who, while accepting the moral and social standards of Christianity, are unable to accept many of its credal statements and forms of worship. This movement, which calls itself "Religionless Christianity", seeks to create the bridge by accepting as proved the scientific world outlook of today, and bases itself upon the alleged fact that "this generation has opted for the secular and has done with the supernatural". Such an approach to the problem is the very antithesis of that of Rudolf Steiner, with his revelation of the reality of the supersense-perceptible, and its essential relevance to the Deed of Christ, to the Christian Gospel, and to the Destiny of Man.

To all these problems Anthroposophy has specific answers, but it has received no serious consideration by the Churches. It is either casually dismissed by the traditional theological substitute for impartial judgement, as "the revival of a long disproved heresy"; or it is rejected on the ground of some startling or unfamiliar item of belief, taken out of its context, and with no consideration or even knowledge of the basic principles on which it rests.

In point of fact, the Churches are not to-day so completely averse to supersensible phenomena as they were at the beginning of the century and they regard with sympathetic interest the study, under approved control, of spiritualism and spirit-healing. But these movements provide only empirical evidence of spirit reality, and the rationale of their belief is very largely speculation. It is all the more surprising that the Churches should show no interest in Anthroposophy, a rationally articulated world-outlook, based on the reality and activity of spirit and derived from direct perception. This perception is based upon the development of inherent organs of supersensible perception by methods which are exactly described, and which involve penetration in full consciousness into different levels of soul experience, factually linked with each other. In the understanding of these levels of experience we arrive at the understanding of the great mysteries of man and of space and time.

In speaking of the Christian Churches I have deliberately made no reference to "The Christian Community", for that Church came into being in 1922 as the expression in a Christian Church of the teaching of Anthroposophy, in despair at the indifference and opposition of the traditional Churches. This Church has a large membership in Germany; in English-speaking countries it is small, but quietly and steadily growing. It manifests a new understanding of the Christian verities in the light of Anthroposophy. But for the traditional Christian Churches the path of discovery of the message of Anthroposophy is not, at first, through its direct interpretation of Christian doctrine, whether in the practice and worship of the Christian Community, or in Dr. Steiner's lectures on the Gospels and on the life and work of Jesus Christ. To do that is to be confronted immediately with statements that may seem to contradict long-accepted views, without any knowledge of the principles on which they are based.

Through his direct experience of spirit and by thorough penetration of this experience by clear thought and honest judgement, Steiner arrived at certain fundamental principles that underlie the whole of man and the universe. Some of these are new, some are a clarification of ancient instinctive knowledge. Some of them challenge accepted scientific and theological conceptions, but they do so in a scientific way. Steiner urged repeatedly that none of these principles should be accepted on authority, but that they should be tested, either by developing in oneself the power of direct spirit-perception, or by submitting them to the most searching tests in the light of existing indisputable factual knowledge. They are, however, so fundamental to his whole world-outlook that it is only comprehensible in the light of them. Moreover, if they are true, they so vitally concern the thinking and life of humanity, that nothing can be more important than an honest consideration of them.

The first principle is the apprehension of the objective reality of spirit, a vast, inter-related supersensible world of spirit-being, existing behind and functioning through material reality, the Alpha and Omega of physical, sense-perceived existence. Such a concept should not be unfamiliar to Christians, who speak in their services every Sunday of "Cherubim and Seraphim", "the heavens and all the powers therein". In spite of this, however, any real living relationship to heavenly spirit is almost non-existent in their minds. Natural Science is governed by the principle of not treating as factual anything that is not capable of being proved by sense-perceptible experiment, but already there is a gathering mass of evidence of events that do not admit of a scientific explanation of this sort. Moreover, if such a world of spirit does exist, it cannot, by its very nature, be subject to sense-derived proof.

The second principle that runs through the whole relation between the spiritual and the physical worlds is that of "Descent and Ascent". For the past hundred years Science has been fascinated by and absorbed in the picture of "Ascent" manifest in the physical world. With varying views as to the motive power in this ascent, the picture remains as a process which had its origin in the lowest physical forms and will have its conclusion in the highest. But Dr. Steiner has revealed the whole process as a continuous "descent" of spirit into matter, shaping first its own being in the supersensible world to the needs of descent, and then evolving a material medium which it progressively shaped more and more adequately to its self-manifestation in physical form. The natural scientific approach is like that of examining the pictures of a great painter, and deciding how they could be arranged in an order of objective artistic merit, and what explanation could be given from the pictures themselves of their artistic advance. It would be seen as a manifest "ascent". The Anthroposophical approach would be to regard the pictures as the progressive "ascending" expression of the artist's creative imagination continually "descending" into pictorial form, how he trained his imagination towards self-expression and by adaptation and new discovery he made his material more and more capable of expressing his genius, a process of descent and ascent continuously repeated at every stage of advance. Whenever there is life in the physical world this process is continuously repeated, in a rhythm of descent ascent and withdrawal; and where, in man, spirit itself completely and consciously descends into the material medium, the process resolves itself into the next great principle that is fundamental to Anthroposophy; the principle of reincarnation, or successive earth-lives.

The belief in reincarnation is one to which the Christian Churches are instinctively opposed, partly because it is not an explicit element in the teaching of Christ, and partly because it has long been regarded as one of the mistaken beliefs of Eastern religions. In point of fact the Eastern conception of reincarnation is quite different from that presented in Anthroposophy. The Eastern religions, based as they were on a primeval human clairvoyance, spoke out of a direct perception of a previous existence. But to them man's lives on earth are a calamity, an exile from his true spirit-existence, and he seeks to bring to an end their repetition by asceticism. But Dr. Steiner explains reincarnation as the necessary application to the individual man of the principle of descent and ascent manifest in the whole universe. It is the spiral of spiritual evolution, by which man is enabled by purgation and spiritual re-integration finally to carry the purpose of his earthly incarnation into pure spirit-existence. In recent years, there has been among Western people a growing interest in the possibility of reincarnation, but it has tended to concentrate all interest and importance on the repeated earth lives, and to fail to realise the process as a great rhythm of being, in which the earth-lives are held together in an unbroken chain of moral consequence, the goal of which lies in the spiritual world.

It is impossible within the scope of this article to consider the relevance of this belief to the Christian Faith, why it was necessary that for nearly two thousand years, while man was achieving an ever deeper knowledge of himself and his material environment, it should be hidden from his consciousness; how vitally important that at this moment in his evolution he should recover that knowledge; how deeply relevant to its needs is the redeeming work of Christ; how it answers many of the apparently inscrutable inequalities of human life and opportunity; and how significant to each one of us it makes, not only our own present earthly existence, but the whole history of man and the earth. Indeed, if reincarnation is true there is no fact that is more vitally urgent to-day for man to apprehend. It leads directly to the next fundamental principle of Anthroposophy, the nature of the being of man in his earthly existence.

The concept of the nature of man governs the thinking and the life of humanity. The greatest menace of our age is the utterly false view of man implicit in materialistic science, and blatantly explicit in Marxian Communism. In Spiritual Science earthly man is seen as a physical-spiritual being. His eternal self, which moves as spirit through this repeated rhythm of being, dwells in each earth-life in a soul-element of thinking, feeling and willing that it has fashioned out of its earth-existences; in a life-element, that brings it from spirit life to conscious inner experience in a continuous time-existence, and finally, in a physical body, a controlled spatial existence, in which alone man can realise himself in moral freedom. Dr. Steiner shows the interplay of these elements in man's being on earth, both when awake and asleep, and in the spiritual life after death.

In one sense this revelation of the true being of man is the very core of the revelation of Rudolf Steiner, as is implicit in the strange-sounding name of his movement. For "Anthroposophy" is the wisdom attained through the discovery of the true nature of man. For the Church it must be of vital importance, for, as we said earlier, there is a widespread tendency to-day to combine a profession of Christian faith with the modern scientific view of man.

This true view of man was unconsciously and only partially present in ancient religions, but since the time of Aristotle man has lost any direct awareness of it. In the first three centuries of Christianity an attempt was made to express the Christian faith in terms of it , but from the fourth century it faded away. It is not too much to say that most of the great theological disputes which have torn the Church asunder since that time have been due to the ignorance on both sides of the true nature of man.

This understanding leads directly to the next great principle explicit in Anthroposophy, the meaning of History. This is a problem which has pressed urgently upon men's minds in the last fifty years. Here again Dr. Steiner saw the working of this great principle of "Descent and Ascent". Here the rhythm is as long as the whole course of human evolution. Slowly man descended from an unself-conscious spirit existence, into gradual incarnation into a material existence. More and more deeply the human race has penetrated into material knowledge and experience, with a corresponding loss of awareness of spirit. From that depth man is slowly ascending, but for that he needs a reawakened spiritual consciousness. The question for our day is whether that consciousness will be blinded by the dazzling splendour of man's latest material discoveries.

The external course of history, the rise and fall of civilisations, the gradual advance in physical knowledge and power from the Stone Age to the Atomic Age, are only half the tale of human history, and can only be properly understood as an element in man's spiritual devolution and evolution. In this long slow rhythm, the quicker rhythm of the individual is not only the necessary condition whereby he may survive the stress and incomprehensibility of the slower movement, but provides, through the return of the spiritually-quickened power of great lives, the impulse which leads to new civilisations.

Perhaps the most striking point and the one most relevant to the Christian Churches is the place which Dr. Steiner gave in this cosmic view of history to the Deed of Christ, the Incarnation. To him it was not only the intervention of God into human history, bringing forgiveness and the hope of immortality to the individual believer, and drawing out a redeemed community from a doomed world. It was the central point of all human history, occurring at the very nadir of mankind's spiritual descent, and bringing new spiritual forces and creative possibilities for the whole future of the spiritual destiny of man. He saw the incarnation not as a sudden deed erupting into history, but as a gradual descent through the levels of existence from spirit to matter, a descent of which great human spirits were aware at different levels and which they expressed in the great religions of mankind, but which found its fulfilment only in Christ. This picture of the Cosmic Christ, the Christ of human destiny, can be the answer to the new race-prejudice, which sees Christianity as a Western ideology.

Anthroposophy proclaims to human thinking the objective and immediate reality of spirit. It also restores to the study of Christian documents and origins the reality of the supersensible. In its light the Bible takes on a new spiritual and rational meaning, the accounts of the Creation and the Fall, the call of Abraham and the segregation of the Hebrew people, the task of Moses, the nature of prophecy, the deep significance of the Exile, the Messianic expectation. So too the New Testament, the deep mystic significance of the four Gospels in their varied presentation, the meaning of Apocalypse. This new understanding of the Bible, based on the teaching of Rudolf Steiner, has been set out with great erudition and spiritual insight by the late Dr. Emil Bock of the Christian Community, in his studies on the Old and New Testaments.

But the chief possibility that lies in an unprejudiced approach to Anthroposophy by the Christian Churches is that with which we began, a real reconciliation of Science and Religion. If the Church can see the work of Christ and the spiritual destiny and redemption of man as involved in the whole evolutionary process; and if Science can see the evolutionary process in the light of its spiritual origin, nature and destiny; then it might begin to happen. That was the task to which Rudolf Steiner devoted his life.

Nineteen centuries ago Saul of Tarsus, a gifted man of about forty, deeply versed in the culture and religious thought of his age, yet wholly committed to the most definite and uncompromising religion of the world, the Jewish faith, had a vision of Christ. As a result of the spiritual initiation which flowed from it, Saul, now become Paul, transformed what was then only a Jewish sect into a world-religion. That involved for him, and for all Jewish Christians, the surrender of religious convictions and rites of the Jewish faith, which had behind them undoubted divine authority,—circumcision, the strict observance of the Jewish Sabbath, the keeping of the whole law of Moses. No greater renunciation of belief, previously held as essential, has ever been made in response to a divine revelation of wider spiritual possibilities.

When he too was about the same age, Rudolf Steiner had an experience of Christ which cannot be better expressed than in his own words: "I stood before the Mystery of Golgotha in a most inward, most solemn festival of knowledge." He too was versed in the scientific and philosophic culture of his day, but also, quite uniquely, in the direct experience of the objective reality of spirit. This he saw as a divinely ordered opportunity for a great advance in the spiritual evolution of humanity, and at the heart of it—the only possibility of its realisation—a new understanding of the Deed of Christ for mankind. Like Paul, he "was not disobedient to the heavenly vision". He saw it as the divine revelation of the possibility of a great renewal of the Christ-Impulse in the life of humanity.

The acceptance of this view of the Christ of human destiny might involve the Churches in the renunciation and readaptation of some forms and beliefs that, in the evolution of Christianity in the Western world, have come to be regarded as fixed. But that renunciation would be far less than that which was involved in the birth of Christianity. The message of Anthroposophy is a challenge and an opportunity which the Christian Churches should face in the deepest seriousness.

# THE TRINITY IN MAN AND NATURE[15]

In this article I am attempting to expound a concept of the nature of Being and Reality that has been in my mind for the past eighteen years. I shall be covering ground that many have explored and written about, but for the most part I shall make little reference to other points of view. To present a subject such as this in one article must involve omissions and tentative statements, but I hope I shall succeed in making plain the general theme of my argument.

As every student of Anthroposophy knows Dr. Steiner revealed the presence in Man and Nature of many trinities or threefold relationships. Man is spirit, soul and body; in his earthly life he functions through three sheaths, the astral, the etheric and the physical; he expresses himself in thinking, and feeling and willing. In his physical manifestation he is head-man, heart-man and limbs and metabolic-man; in his path to Higher Knowledge he experiences three higher levels of consciousness and being, Imagination, Inspiration and Intuition. In Nature again there are three levels of consciousness and being—in the mineral kingdom, the plant kingdom and the animal kingdom.

In this article I do not intend to dwell on the workings of these trinities in Man and Nature, but rather upon the concept of Trinity itself, in its relation to Man and Nature; the concept of Trinity in Unity, and Unity in Trinity, which in this form of expression is familiar to us in the Christian definition of the Godhead, as set out in the Athanasian Creed. There the two sides of the seeming paradox are stated in the most precise terms, with no attempt to explain or reconcile them, but simply as a fundamental dogma of faith. What I seek to maintain is that this apparent paradox of Trinity in Unity and Unity in Trinity is not a mere theological deduction from divine revelation, but is—as we might have expected it to be, if we really believe it to be the nature of the Godhead—a revelation of the true nature of all being and reality.

*     *     *

In setting out this thesis, I propose to start from the level of universal sense-experience and of scientific thinking, from the age-long perplexity of modern thought as to the nature of Man's perception through his senses of the world around him. In the naïve view of the ordinary man, his visual sense-perception gives him a direct, objective awareness of objects

---

15 Originally given as a lecture at the members' conference of the Anthroposophical Society in Great Britain; Ripon, July 1959. Then published in The Golden Blade 1960.

outside himself, and he regards what is given in sense-perception—colour, form, etc.—as the properties of the object perceived, correcting and balancing the evidence of his eyes by that of his other senses.

The scientific thinker, tracing the physical process of visual perception—as far as he can trace it—holds that we perceive only an inner picture, created by the brain, which bears no direct revelation of the nature of the object "perceived", although it is adequate as a practical means of relating ourselves to it.

I do not intend in this article to investigate the process of sense-perception, intensely important though it is. Rudolf Steiner spoke a great deal about it, and I believe that the point of view I am trying to establish would throw great light upon it. But all that I am concerned with now is the fact of sense-experience.

This image that we perceive, whatever be the process by which we perceive it, is rooted in both the perceiver and the perceived. It is a relation to each other in which they stand. The picture which I have of a rose depends upon the presence of a rose within the visual range of my eyes. If the rose is taken away, or if I turn my back upon it, the image disappears. Neither I nor the rose can claim the image for itself, for it does not exist except as a relationship between us.

This would seem to challenge the assertion that the image is "created" by the brain. At best, the image is an interpretation of received impressions. The brain cannot create any other sort of picture from those sense-impressions than the one it arrives at, and it continually tests and corrects this picture by reference to the received impressions, and those of other senses. Visual sense-experience, therefore, is a relationship between the perceiver and the perceived.

Here I want to make a most important point. This relationship is vital to both perceiver and perceived, not only as a useful process of knowledge, a means of communication, but vital also to their *being*, their *existence*. The image of the rose—the fact that I see the rose as red—is part of what I *am*. The fact that the rose, in that relation to me, appears as red is part of what the rose *is*.

＊　　＊　　＊

Let us develop this a little further, beginning with my claim that my perceived image of the rose is part of what I am, of my very being. Man's self does not consist merely of his immediate momentary physical existence, but of his continuous inner experience. When I say "I" in the deepest sense, I do not refer to the former but to the latter, my inner experience, which is preserved and is, in a measure, recoverable in memory, and is more deeply and completely preserved in my etheric body, or, in terms of psychology, my "Unconscious". If the whole of my sense-experience of the outer world of Nature and Man is taken away from this inner self of continuous experience, what is left? Quite obviously this relationship between myself and the outer world, which expresses itself through sense-experience, is a vital element in my being. Of course there are other relationships between myself and the world about me, some of them physical and obvious, others of which I am unconscious. But the fact remains that the visual images which I have in perception, and all the impressions I receive through my senses, are, in a very real sense, part of my being.

It is perhaps less obvious and not so easy to demonstrate that this relationship is also part of the being of the perceived object. For it has been the aim of the philosophy and science of the last four centuries to seek in the object perceived for the "thing-in-itself", behind and independent of its appearance to the observer. The qualities which arise in sense-perception as a relationship between the observer and the thing observed were defined as secondary qualities, and were disregarded as relevant only to the observer and no part of the reality of the object observed. Investigation was concentrated on the so-called primary qualities, which were held to be independently inherent in the object itself, such as weight, size, etc. But these qualities are no less a relationship than the discarded "secondary qualities". If any object were the only object in the world, no conclusion could be arrived at about its weight or size, for these can be conceived and expressed only in comparison with other objects. It is a relationship to these objects.

The discoveries of nuclear science show that atomic structure—the foundation of matter—does not reveal a material "thing-in-itself", but only a rigidly controlled relationship of electron, proton and neutron, themselves only focal points in fields of force. In a recent article in the *Sunday Times* on "The Elementary Particles within the Atom", Professor Salam says: "Each one of these particles exists in interaction with certain others". Indeed, it has been one of the discoveries of nuclear science that at a certain stage the observer himself cannot be detached from the object under consideration; the very fact that he is "observing" has a direct effect upon the object under observation. The basis of matter itself is relationship.

Furthermore, to disregard the "secondary qualities" manifest in sense-perception is to disregard the fundamental relationships in which the object stands to the observer, relationships far more essential to its particular manifested being than are the nuclear relationships which underlie it. For example, if a rose is reduced to its material elements or its atomic structure—in which there is neither colour, scent, nor form, as manifested in sense-experience—then the rose, as a rose, is no longer there; just as the dissection of an Old Master into classified particles of canvas and paint is no longer a picture, and its whole *raison d'être* has been destroyed. As George Macdonald wrote: "The show, the appearance of things, is that for which God cares most... It is through their show, not through their analysis, that we enter into the deepest relationship to them."

In point of fact, do we not build up the reality of any object by discovering more and more of the relationships in which it stands, to ourselves, to other objects, or within is own manifested being? All these we build up by thought working upon our sense-impressions, for none of these relationships is directly manifest in bare sense-impressions. First, we discover, by thought, the relationships of colour and form in which the visual sense-impressions present themselves, and verify or elaborate them by other sense-impressions, of sound or touch, etc. Then we go on by thought, to further relationships not directly given in the sense-impressions. These relationships we build into the reality of the object so completely that, having become familiar with it, we come to think of this whole complex of relationships almost as directly given in the sense-impressions. But the fact remains that the reality of the object consists entirely of relationships discovered by thought.

Indeed, it is interesting to see how, even to the thinker, the wider reality, which includes discovered relationships not apparent in the sense-impressions themselves, appears to manifest itself directly to sense-perception. This can be seen in such a programme on television as "Animal Vegetable or Mineral", if one watches the face of, let us say, Sir Mortimer Wheeler as he takes into his hands some article or even fragment of pottery. He receives from it the same sense-impression as would be given to anyone else, but as one watches in his eyes the intense thought with which he scrutinises the object, it would almost appear as though the manifold relationships of place and date and probable form and use, derived from thought and stored-up in his memory, have become directly manifest to his sense-experience, as composing the reality of that at which he is looking.

It should be noted that the claim that the relationship given in sense-perception is part of the reality of both observer and observed is not invalidated by the fact that to a colour-blind person the object appears in what we should call "the wrong colour". For this fact, that the rose appears in this colour to the colour-blind person, is still part of the rose's reality, as it is also part of the reality of the colour-blind observer.

Thus we see, not only that the reality of any object consists in its relationships discovered by observation and thought, but that there is no part of the being of the object that is not a relationship, either to entities outside itself, or to entities discoverable within itself. This also seems to be supported by the latest discoveries of nuclear science. In the article by Professor Salam already referred to, he says of the "neutron" that it can exist only in relationship to another particle. "When left free, a neutron decays in about ten minutes into a proton, an electron and a neutrino." He concludes with a startling statement. "The elusive neutrino, a massless, electrically neutralised particle, is perhaps the most perfect instance of a disembodied spirit"! He might have said, "of a pure relationship".

Hence we must say that entities consist of relationships, are built up out of relationships. Relationships are the substance of existence and being. This applies equally to conscious entities, such as animals, and self-conscious entities, such as men or spirit-beings. Between self-conscious beings, of course, consciousness itself enters into the relationships, and lifts them to a new level, producing also a new level of being. Yet the fact remains that the relationships constitute the reality of the beings.

We have already considered how this truth applies to unconscious objects, but there is more to be said in regard to this. So intricate and yet ordered is the pattern of relationships in the object, so integrated with our own conscious thinking, that one is driven to the conclusion that the objects are the expression of conscious beings behind the phenomenon, with whom the relationship and its consequent reality may well be an even more vivid experience than it is to us. One is reminded of the satirical question and answer of the late Monsignor Ronald Knox:

> *The Question. "There once was a man who*
> *said: 'God*
> *Must think it exceedingly odd*
> *That the sycamore tree*
> *Continues to be*

*When there's no-one about in the*
*Quad.'"*
*The Answer. "Dear Sir, Your astonishment's*
*odd:*
*I am always about in the quad,*
*And that's why the tree*
*Continues to be,*
*Since observed by Yours faithfully, God."*

As St. Paul put it, "God is not far from any one of us; for in Him we live and move and have our being."

But the fact that the relationship is a constituent in the being of both entities to which it relates has a profound effect on the nature of the relationship itself, and of the trinity of which it forms a part. The relationship itself can never be regarded as "abstract", because it is the constituent of the entities to which it relates, and therefore itself partakes of the nature of their "being". Moreover, inasmuch as this quality of "being" expressed in the relationship is shared by each of its participants, the subject, the object and the actualised relationship, and also cannot be possessed by any of them alone—for its existence presupposes all three— we have here a trinity, in which each is itself an entity, and yet all three are united in a unity of being. This I call Trinitarian Reality and Being.

\*     \*     \*

But we have not yet exhausted the nature and significance of these relationships which our thinking discovers. Not only do they constitute the very being of the objects which they link together, and in that measure themselves partake of "being", but the relationships themselves can become entities independent of that relationship, a new point of being from which fresh relationships establish themselves in ever-widening creativity.

The rose-colour, which manifests itself as a relationship between the rose and myself becomes itself an entity of colour, establishing a new range of related entities of colour, independent of that particular relationship. Relationships are therefore seen, not only as constituents of being, but as the creative source of new entities.

This is manifest in perhaps the greatest achievement of human thinking, the science of mathematics. This is a science entirely of relationships. Objects are necessary as focal points of relationship, but they are undefined, and presented symbolically as x or y. This science of relationships, carried to more and more complicated and abstruse heights, beyond the range of the ordinary mind, has manifested the creative quality of relationships, in that mathematics has been the key to many of the deepest secrets of science and the instrument of its greatest discoveries and of its ventures into new fields of knowledge and achievement.

Thus, what appears at first sight in our sense-experience as a duality of subject and object, or object and object, each of whose being is explained by abstract relationships with the other, becomes a trinity of subject, object and relationship, in which relationship, contributing to and partaking of the reality of both subject and object, has itself become an entity, and, in so doing, ever creatively extends this Trinitarian Reality.

\* \* \*

All this points to the doctrine of the Trinity with which we started, but we have not yet exhausted the analogy. For this doctrine is not only of a Trinity of Persons, whose being and consciousness share in the identity of their mutual relationships. This Trinity of Being is also a Unity of Being which includes the whole, and is thus shared in and experienced as a whole by each and all of the Persons of the Trinity.

Now is there any human experience which bears analogy to this all-inclusive experience of Unity and Trinity? It must be an experience which includes consciousness of the self as a focal point of relationships, yet feels itself expanded into a consciousness of wider being, which includes itself and all the beings to which it is related, and also the relationships between them.

There is, in the first place, the mystical experience to which many mystics have borne witness: a sense of expansion of being, until it appears to be all-inclusive—and yet, with all these, an experience of being far more intense than personal, individual self-consciousness. There is a similar pattern of experience quite frequently in Christian conversion, a sense of expansion in a new-found love of the whole world. It is expressed in the words of Saul Kane the suddenly converted drunken boxer in Masefield's *Everlasting Mercy*:

> *"I knew that Christ had given me birth*
> *To brother all the souls on earth,*
> *And every bird and every beast*
> *Should share the crumbs broke at the feast."*

So, too, in Intuition, the last stage of Higher Knowledge, as Rudolf Steiner describes it, there is the experience of mutual interpenetration of being, each experiencing himself in the other and the other in himself, passing on to the experience of sharing in all-inclusive reality, with intensified consciousness of self.

109

To conceive of this profound Trinitarian Reality in concepts is almost impossible. Perhaps, we may try to form an Imagination of it, conscious that such a picture must fall far short of the reality.

Let us picture a vast transparent sphere filled with an endless network of criss-crossing threads of relationship. Wherever they meet is an object. Where many threads meet, is a focal point of being. At the centre and pervading the whole is the Godhead, the perfect mutual relationship of Father, Son and Holy Spirit, out of whose personified creativity all these myriad relationships have come and keep coming into being.

From our perception of the working of Trinitarian reality at the level of our physical consciousness, we are able to realise more clearly the significance of the Triune Godhead. Relationship being the essence of true being, we see the eternal necessity of at least a dual personal consciousness within the Godhead itself—The Father, the Ground and Source of all Being, and the Son "begotten before the worlds", weaving and creating out of the Divine Substance; the "eternal Word, through whom all things were made".

In this relationship they are not two separate Persons, each experiencing the other, but the relationship and experience are always "two-way"—"I in the Father and the Father in Me". What the Son is to the Father is part of the being of the Father; it is also part of the being of the Son. What the Father is to the Son is part of the Son; it is also part of the being of the Father. "I and the Father are one." And this pulse of being between the Father and the Son, which is Divine Life, constituting as it does the essence of their being, is Itself personal, the Eternal Spirit "proceeding from the Father and Son", providing the threads of true relationship by which the Son creates.

In this Tri-Personal Unity of Being the Godhead consists, and, out of the joy and blessedness of its own being, seeks to bring self-consciousness and conscious relation to itself to those focal points of relationship which have in them the potentiality of self-conscious being. To achieve this end, these immature beings must first be withdrawn from their consciousness of existing wholly in this totality of Trinitarian Being. They must be brought into a condition of "separated" consciousness. In this lowered experience they gradually become aware of themselves as focal points of being, which more and more appear to be completely self-contained and separate from other focal points of being, any relationships discovered between themselves and other entities appearing impersonal and abstract, except in so far as they affect their physical being.

Moreover, the relationships perceived extend to a very limited range, of which they themselves seem to be the centre. This is the sphere of physical consciousness.

But when, as by death, physical beings are released from the controlled time-experience of their "separated" consciousness, they discover that their relationships no longer appear abstract, but as the very constituent elements in their being. Moreover, they perceive that these relationships extend ever more widely and deeply through the universal network of being and relationship, and in this experience their own being, now conscious of existing in its relationships, seems to expand so as to include the whole sphere of being. Finally, they experience the relationships which unite them to the Godhead itself and so reach consciously the level of Trinitarian being, at which level they and other beings experience themselves and one another in interpenetration of universal being.

\* \* \*

What I have tried to show so far is that the doctrine of the divine Trinity in Unity and Unity in Trinity is not a mere theological concept—as some believe—but that it is a revelation of the real nature of all being; indeed, of all reality. Also that indications of this are given in the universal experience of sense-perception and knowledge, and, to a still greater degree, in mystic and super-sensory experience. What I would now attempt to show is how this conception permeates and is implicit in Dr. Steiner's teaching.

Let us begin with that which was the earliest element in his teaching, the nature of man's knowledge of the world through sense-perception as it is set out in *"The Philosophy of Spiritual Activity"*. We have already considered man's sense-experience as containing fundamental elements of Trinitarian Reality, but this is all the more evident as we consider the light which Dr. Steiner threw on this subject.

He revealed, in a quite new way, the fundamental place of thought in sense-perception, and pointed out how rarely the thinking man — and still less the ordinary man — "thinks about thinking". He pointed out that man's awareness of the reality about him had been "split asunder": part was given to man in sense-impressions, but man has himself to bring to bear upon these his own activity of thinking, and only in this way establishes conscious relationships with reality. Thus thinking is a spiritual activity, an activity of man as spirit.

When we apply to this the concept of Trinitarian Reality, we see that what man seeks in thinking is to discover relationships between his

111

diverse sense-impressions, and between the so-perceived separate objects of sense-experience. Some time ago I heard Sir Julian Huxley say, in a television broadcast, that what he would most like to know of things not yet known was, "What is thinking?" I would venture to suggest the answer: "Thinking is the search for and application of relationships implicit in and between objects of sense-experience."

Moreover, man thinks, not only because relationships complete knowledge, and provide means of contact, but because *they complete his being*. In order that he may acquire self-awareness, man finds himself, not only with a divided knowledge, but with a divided *being*. Sense-impressions give him an awareness of entities outside his separated, self-contained physical self. They can be made real only by establishing relationships between them and one another and himself. Moreover, he can only complete his own reality as a spirit being by establishing these relationships with the world impinging on him. *Thinking then is the pathway to spirit-being.* Man thinks because he needs relationships in order to live, and in a "separated" existence he must look for them. His spirit would starve if it could not establish relationships between itself and other entities.

But the relationships found in this way are not "compelling", as they are in the spiritual world. They appear, to the ordinary man, as abstract thoughts, revealing the nature of separated objects outside himself. They leave him free to accept or reject, to use or misuse them. But if man would rise to his full heritage, he must discover in full consciousness the Trinitarian reality of subject and object in living relationship, as constituting the true reality and being, both of himself, and of each and all of the "separated" objects.

&ast;  &ast;  &ast;

We find indications of the concept of Trinitarian reality also in Dr. Steiner's exposition of how the three stages of Higher Knowledge, Imagination, Inspiration and Intuition are reached. The first stage, "Imagination", is reached by directing concentrated meditation upon a spiritual reality of whose existence we are aware, but which is not manifest to our sense-experience, as, for example, the growth-forces of a plant. If the meditation is successful, the spiritual reality makes an impression on us, through our developed soul-organs of perception, in form and colour. This is an "Imagination". It is, as it were, a spiritual sense-impression giving an awareness of a spirit-object impressing this pattern of form and colour upon us. But as yet we do not know the nature of that object itself, but only its effect upon ourselves. For us to know it, it must itself establish a direct relationship with us, which will reveal its own being.

We have, therefore, to dismiss form our attention the "Imagination"— that is, the effect which the object made upon ourselves from without— and wait until we receive from the spirit-reality a communication of the relationship which links it to ourselves. We wait in pure thought-meditation, directing our relationship-discovering faculty of thought towards the object, until, as Spinoza put it, "spirit comes to meet us". This is the stage of "Inspiration", the stage of the discovery of spirit-reality itself in revealed relationships, and the discovery that in those relationships not only the spirit-reality, but we ourselves, consist.

Then, when relationship is fully taken up into being, we reach the final stage of "Intuition", where living in relationship passes into a mutual interpenetration of being, an experience of oneself in the other, and the other in oneself. Subject Object and Relationship have been taken up into Trinitarian Being.

*　　*　　*

These three stages of Higher Knowledge are, of course, only an anticipation, by the path of spiritual self-development, of the actual ascent of the human spirit after death, first through the etheric realm of picture-consciousness or spirit-awareness, then to the astral realm of living in the moral discovery of the ontological significance of relationships; and finally to the pure spirit-realm of Trinitarian being. This repeated ascent and descent of the stairway of being between spiritual and earthly consciousness, leading from earth-life to earth-life, is not only the pathway of individual spirit-evolution, but through the reincarnation of great spirits it provides the impulse for the gradual spiritual evolution on earth of mankind—from unconscious Trinitarian being, through separated being, to full separated self-consciousness, and finally, by rediscovery of the reality of spirit, to fully-conscious Trinitarian being.

In a very illuminating way Dr. Steiner shows how this spiritual evolution of mankind has worked out in human history. For he shows that the key to understanding of human history is not to be found primarily in man's gradual discovery and mastery of the physical world, but in the evolution of human consciousness in that process. In this we find the clearest indication of presence and working of Trinitarian reality.

Descending from an unself-conscious Trinitarian existence in universal being, in his earliest contact with the physical world man still felt deeply the unity between his own being and the other beings and entities, spiritual and physical, about him. He lived in vivid

113

consciousness of vital relationships between himself and them, in the light of which he interpreted their being. He was as yet hardly aware of his or their separate existence.

Gradually this original experience began to fade into a more "separated" consciousness, in which man looked for guidance to the leaders of the Mystery-centres, who still retained spiritual vision and understanding. It was an age of ever-expanding experience and development of physical existence, but one in which man still felt himself linked with the spirit-world, his fellow-men, and the world about him. It was the age of the *Sentient Soul*.

With the rise of Greek civilisation man entered into a new stage of "separated" existence. He became more and more conscious of his own being at one end of his experience—that is, of himself as *Subject*, able not only to experience, but to initiate and control relationships with external entities, and as having moral responsibility in doing so. It was the age of the *Intellectual Soul, the Subject-conscious Soul*; and the "I", as subject, became increasingly interested in itself and its possibilities. Nevertheless, for centuries man still retained a consciousness of being linked with the world about him.

Four centuries ago, with the dawn of the scientific age, man became supremely interested in that which was at the other end of his experience, the *Object*, disregarding his own personal relationship to it, and considering it wholly in its relationship to other objects. Relationships still remain, but they no longer deeply affect him, nor, for the most part, hold any moral content for him. They are simply abstract laws, a method of gaining knowledge and control of objects. It is the age of *the Consciousness-Soul, the Object-conscious Soul*; Nature is utterly devoid of spirit and is regarded merely as an object of exploitation, for which man has no sense of responsibility. In this concentration upon Object-consciousness man has included himself as an object equally with other material objects, a phenomenon of the physical world, governed by abstract laws. The trustworthiness of man in his subject-activity is questioned, even his right as an ordinary individual to exercise such a function at all.

Finally, in this twentieth century the emphasis has gradually shifted from Object-consciousness to *Relationship-consciousness*. We have already referred to higher mathematics as the science of abstract relationships and to the discoveries in nuclear science of relationships as the basis of matter. The significance of Subject and Object, of man and the world he lives in, seems lost in the incomprehensible abstract mathematical relationships by which the high-priests of the Science-Mysteries explain them. Moreover, these supposedly abstract relationships have been able to release and to create forces which threaten, not only the harmony of existence, but existence itself. Nor is it only in pure science that the worship of relationships in themselves has been set up. Political and social ideologies, economic world-schemes and industrial set-ups, wholesale educational systems, have become dominant relationships, in which the individual subject or object are mere pawns and their significance almost irrelevant.

It is the opposite process to that of Higher Knowledge. The wheel has gone full circle from the all-embracing Trinitarian Unity of the Spirit-world. Subject and object and one object and another object are seen as separate entities, and the former living relationships between them have become either properties of the objects, or merely abstract laws, or impersonal fields of force that threaten the existence of both subject and object. Man is left wondering if there is any vital relation at all between subject and object, between himself and the world.

* * *

There are, however, indications of a reaction against mere despair. Science, as we have seen, is beginning to realise that relationships cannot be treated as abstractions, but are a concrete factor in reality, even relationships between observer and observed. So, too, there is a growing conviction that political ideologists must not be allowed to function in disregard of the well-being of individuals and their way of life; that uninhibited economic competition cuts its own throat; that the disregard of the natural aspirations and needs of undeveloped peoples must breed wars; and, finally, that only in co-operation with the laws of Nature's own being can man depend on her sustenance.

But these experience-bought readjustments of human living cannot of themselves solve the problem. Man must return from his "separated" consciousness to an awareness of Trinitarian reality. In order that he might do so in full consciousness, it was necessary for him first to acquire his separated awareness of the three elements in that inclusive reality, Subject, Object and Relationship, even as in the Godhead itself the triple personal consciousness is necessary for the experience of the Triune Unity.

Although he is unconscious of it, man is a microcosm of the macrocosm of the Godhead. But he can only be a real, self-conscious centre of spirit-being, a spirit-self, by a mutual subject-object and object-subject relationship between himself and God, and between himself and the created world, which is the expression, through the hierarchies, of the Divine Word. To obtain Trinitarian being, this relationship must be reciprocal, as it is between the Persons in the Godhead. Man's great mistake has been to regard his relationships as only one-way—from himself, both in regard to the created world and even towards his fellow men; to disregard the other man's point of view, and, in any case, not to recognise it as of any ontological significance to his own being. He must learn to allow his spirit to be "object" to the speaking of others and also to the speaking of the created world. Man cannot reach this all-inclusive unity of being out of a separated, materialistic outlook, devoid of spirit. He must press on, with the aid of Spiritual Science, to the actual discovery of spirit, if he is to attain the true nature of Trinitarian being.

But it is in the work of Christ for mankind, on which Dr. Steiner gave some of his most illumining revelations, that the real working in heaven and earth of the Trinitarian Mystery is most apparent. In a quite unique series of books and lectures, Dr. Steiner revealed the deed of Christ in Incarnation, in its divinely-planned relationship to the whole spiritual evolution of mankind.

The descent of Christ into the physical life of humanity took place at the moment when man was about to enter the final stage of the "separation" of his consciousness. The intellectual or subject-conscious soul was beginning to lose its instinctive sense of connection with the world about it, and in a few centuries, after a period of bewilderment, it would change into the complete "separatedness" of the Consciousness-Soul, the Object-conscious Soul.

Christ could not arrest this evolution of consciousness, because, until man had discovered himself in "separatedness", he could not consciously enter into the true experience of his being in Trinitarian relationship. But what Christ was not yet able to do for man's Thinking, He was able to do for man's Feeling. Dr. Steiner often speaks of Christ's earthly work as the redemption of man's Feeling, and of the present age as the opportunity to receive through Christ the redemption of man's Thinking.

Christ Himself declared that the one new commandment He had brought to men was that they should love one another, as He had loved them, in giving His life for them. It was not the first time that men had been told to love each other. Love in the ancient world was not a mere emotion. It expressed the perfection of relationship between man and God, and between man and man. When on Mount Sinai, Moses gave the

Law, he transposed the true spiritual relationships, as he could see them in the spirit world, into a code of earthly relationships. He summed it up—as Christ Himself did—as perfect love towards God and towards man. Moreover, Moses revealed the fact that this love, this relationship, was not only a code of conduct, but the very substance of man's being, when he said, " Behold, I have set before you this day good and evil, life and death."

But in the crisis in human history at the coming of Christ, man needed more than a commandment; he needed a Divine example. The love that the Death and Resurrection of Christ awakened in men's hearts passed from feeling into devotion and became, not only a redemption of feeling, but the beginning of the redemption of will. In the experience of it man reached a new level of consciousness and a new level of being.

We find this expressed again and again in St. Paul's Epistles, and especially in the first Epistle of St. John. St. John offers men the eternal life which was with God and had been manifested to men, the new life of relationship to the Father and the Son, through the Spirit of Love which filled them. "That ye may have fellowship with us, and our fellowship is with the Father and with his Son, Jesus Christ." It was a new life, a new experience of being. "We know that we have passed from death unto life, because we love the brethren." It was a new level of consciousness. "He that abideth in love abideth in God, and God abideth in him."

But perhaps the mystery of Trinitarian being and relationship was most completely expressed by Christ Himself in his last great prayer. "I pray that they may all be one: even as thou, Father, art in me and I in thee, that they also may be in us . . . that they may be one, even as we are one; I in them, and thou in me, that they may be brought to perfection into one; that the love where-with thou lovest me may be in them, and I in them."

The method by which this should be achieved is described by Christ as the releasing of man's soul out of the prison of his "separated" experience, by restoring to it again Trinitarian consciousness. "How shall this happen to us," His disciple asked, "and not happen to the world?" "If a man love me," Christ replied, " he will keep my word; and my Father will love him, and we will come unto him and make our abode with him."

Looking down the course of Christian history, it might appear that Christians have completely failed to achieve this Trinitarian Unity. But is it not rather that the conditions for its full realisation have not yet been attained?  Christian feeling and devotion are limited by the fact that man's thinking cannot yet free itself from the Ahrimanic delusion of the ultimate nature of "separated" physical existence.  It is from this delusion that Christ would redeem man's thinking at the present time, by enabling his Christ-filled soul to acquire, through the self-development of Higher Knowledge, a direct experience of spirit-reality.  When man's thinking can grasp the reality of spirit in man and nature, then it will reach that understanding of Trinitarian reality and being which will enable Christ's vision for man to be fulfilled.

But it will not be only man's relationship to God and Man that will be redeemed; with it there will be the long-awaited redemption of Nature of which St. Paul spoke.  For man's soul being delivered by this Christ-given Trinitarian consciousness from the prison of his own astral experience, his Thinking will also be delivered, by the discovery of the reality of spirit, from the Ahrimanic delusion of the permanence of separated physical reality.  Then he will know Nature, not only as mirrored in his own sense-perception, or as the "other ", to be mastered and exploited; but in her own soul-filled, God-related, man-related being. Then the triple polarities of Man and Nature, God and Nature, Man and God will be resolved into the true Trinitarian reality of Nature, Man and God.  Then once again Man will walk with God among the trees of the garden of Nature, because in his Christ-won Trinitarian consciousness he will no longer feel naked and ashamed.

# THE INCARNATION[16]

The Incarnation is the central doctrine of the Christian Faith. "The word was made flesh and dwelt among us." It is a belief that to other religions and to the modern scientific mind is the great stumbling block to the acceptance of Christianity, but without it the Christian gospel loses all its significance. It is expressed in the New Testament in the nativity stories of St. Matthew and St. Luke, but it was not the subject of debate in the early years of the Christian Church. The problems that St. Paul discussed were the Cross and the Resurrection. The divinity of Christ was unquestioned on the living evidence of those who had been witnesses of His Resurrection.

But by the fourth century the subtle minds of the Eastern theologians of the Church began to dispute about the relation of the two natures, human and divine, in Christ, and there followed three centuries of heresies and defining General Councils, in which the confusion of thought was due, not so much to man's ignorance of the being of God, as to his growing ignorance as to the nature of Man himself. By the end of the seventh century the doctrine of the divine-human Christ was settled and was not seriously challenged until the rise of materialistic scientific thought in the nineteenth century.

To turn from theology of the Incarnation to its actual happening in history, the orthodox view bases this upon the nativity accounts in Matthew and Luke; the Annunciation, the divine conception in the virgin's womb—thus in some way escaping the taint of original sin—and finally the birth of the child, who is born; completely and at once, both God and man.

There are obvious difficulties in this historic evidence, for the nativity accounts in Matthew and Luke are almost wholly different. There are two different genealogies, both traced to Joseph, which would seem irrelevant to a virgin birth. The stories are quite different. In Matthew the Annunciation takes place to Joseph in Bethlehem, in Luke it is to Mary and took place at Nazareth. The parents of the Matthew child had their home in Bethlehem, from which they fled to Egypt when the child was about two years old, to escape the wrath of Herod. Returning later, they were directed in a dream to make their home at Nazareth. The parents of the Luke child were natives of Nazareth and the child was born

---

[16] First published in the Anthroposophical Quarterly Vol.4 No.4 Winter 1959.

at Bethlehem on a taxation visit. After a few weeks they all returned to Nazareth. The Matthew child was visited by the three wise Magi of the East; the Luke child by simple shepherds. In fact no single incident is common to both narratives, and no attempt is made in the New Testament to reconcile them.

These discrepancies were perceived from the second century, but they were glossed over by the unquestioning faith in the divine-human nature of Christ. But the rise of scientific thought, with its growing assumption of man as the product of natural evolution from a material origin, has used these discrepancies to discredit the whole belief, and some of the latest theology would dismiss the nativity stories as apocryphal and legendary. This point of view is discounted by the popular religious attachment to the nativity stories, but these are now upheld by the dogmatic belief in the Incarnation, rather than regarded as the evidence that upholds that belief. The latter, moreover, is only held as a necessary corollary to faith in Christ as the divine mediator and redeemer between God and man, without any attempt to understand how and why it so happened or its relation to the whole spiritual evolution of mankind.

Rudolf Steiner, with his spiritual realization that the Incarnation and the Mystery of Golgotha are the pivotal events in the whole historical and psychological evolution of mankind, devoted several books and many lectures to their exposition, and he sets out in detail the background and process of the Incarnation. At first reading his exposition must appear complicated and even incredible, but it will be seen that it is in keeping with the gospel narratives and solves their apparent inconsistencies. It is strange that a scientific age that accepts theories of the origin and nature of the material world that only a few minds can really grasp, should expect profound spiritual events to be patently of a "simple" explanation.

It is impossible, however, to understand Steiner's exposition unless one realizes the great facts about the origin of man and the nature of his evolution on which they are based. These will be familiar to students of Anthroposophy but it will, of course, be impossible in this article to expound or justify them to the general reader. It is necessary, however, to be aware of them as the facts in accordance with which the process of the Incarnation, as Steiner describes it, is to be understood.

In the first place we must remember that Steiner declared again and again that his exposition was not based on written records, nor on hypotheses built upon them, but on the direct investigation of the supersensible record of physical events, which is discoverable by trained spirit-faculties. This has always been known among occultists as the Akashic, or Imperishable, Record. Strange as this must seem to our modern consciousness, we have the witness of two English seers, the seventeenth century poet, Thomas Traherne, and A.E. (G. W. Russell) in this century, that they had frequent direct experience of this imperishable record. It was in comparing the Biblical records with this direct knowledge that Steiner threw light on so many difficult passages in the former.

In the next place Steiner knew by spirit perception that man is a spirit being incarnating in the physical world as a necessary stage in his evolution. Moreover he knew, in relation to this, the fact of reincarnation or recurring earth lives. This long-accepted belief of the ancient religions of the East Steiner saw in quite a new light, in relation, not only to individual salvation but to the whole evolution of mankind. Many thinkers in the West, both secular and Christian, are coming to the conclusion that the evidence for reincarnation is strong, but few realize how completely it alters the problem of human redemption and the process of the Incarnation itself.

Again, with his understanding of man as a fourfold spirit being,[17] physical, etheric, astral and ego, each of which comes to birth successively in every seven years of childhood, Steiner knew that human incarnation is a process, not an event. But though the incarnating spirit being is not actually present in the new-born infant, nonetheless it is shaping this earthly vehicle through which it can express itself and which it will ultimately completely indwell. Such knowledge bears deeply upon the understanding of the divine Incarnation.

Finally Steiner did not see Christianity merely as one of the great world religions. The descent of Christ into the earthly realm was implicit in the whole evolution of mankind and it was seen and spoken of from its earliest days. It was a universal hope and longing, expressed, however inarticulately, in the ancient religions. Steiner shows how in the deed of Incarnation the great religious teachers of the past were involved.

With this background of thought and knowledge in our minds, let us consider how Dr. Steiner expounded this great mystery. In the first place there would be two almost mutually exclusive requirements in regard to

---

17  For a full understanding of Rudolf Steiner's terminology—physical, etheric, astral and ego, see his book "'Theosophy,' an introduction to the supersensible knowledge of the World and the Destination of Man." This and other titles by him are published by Rudolf Steiner Press London.

the physical human organism that was to be the vehicle of Christ, the Divine Ego, who was descending to be the Saviour of mankind. As a result of the Fall, through the ages of heredity and reincarnation the human organism, astral, etheric and physical, had become tainted and impaired by the forces of Lucifer and Ahriman, the spirits of pride and materialism. No such body could contain the Christ, who could only be incarnate in a body free from any such taint. At the same time, the Christ, as Saviour of mankind from this very taint, must in some way enter into the experience of mankind. These two requirements were met in two separate human organisms, which were later to unite to become the human vehicle of the Christ.

As implied in the gospel narratives of Matthew and Luke, there were two different children born for this purpose, one living at Bethlehem and the other at Nazareth, the parents in both cases being named Joseph and Mary. Apart from any specific spiritual provision in this, the names were too common to cause us much surprise. As it is, in the gospel narratives there are two Josephs descended from quite different genealogies, while among the closest women disciples of Jesus two other Marys are specifically mentioned in addition to the mother of Jesus. Both Josephs are descended from King David, the Bethlehem Joseph through Solomon and the royal line, and the Nazareth Joseph through Solomon's brother, Nathan, the less known priestly line.

The necessity that the Incarnation should take place in the Hebrew race is explained by Dr. Steiner. In order that the divine I AM should be able to incarnate at a time when man was still groping towards ego consciousness, it was necessary that a people should experience an ego development in advance of the rest of humanity. In Abraham the foundation of these conditions was laid in his conception of the Deity as the cause of, but wholly other than, the created world, and also as the I AM, in a personal relation, or "covenant," with himself. By an enforced purity of race these qualities in Abraham were passed down though the generations of the Hebrew people and, after forty two generations—as given in the Matthew genealogy—had evolved a physical body in which Jesus could be born.

To each of these two pairs of parents was born a son, who by divine direction was called "Jesus." We shall refer to these two children as "the Nathan Jesus" and the "Solomon Jesus."

The Nathan Jesus provided the pure, untainted organism in which the Christ could dwell. The spirit being incarnating in that child had never before lived on Earth and so had never passed through the process of reincarnation. As the Lucan genealogy shows, in tracing the child's hereditary origin beyond Abraham, beyond Adam, to God Himself, this was the second Adam, a spirit being such as Adam himself had been before the Fall, bringing to earthly birth an astral, an etheric and a spiritual-physical body over which neither Lucifer nor Ahriman had ever had power. Moreover, the child bore within itself the young, fresh, untapped forces of the human being as it had been prepared and equipped in former cosmic states of spiritual evolution for the realization of its ego in earthly incarnation.

The spirit being received its material body from the substance of two parents of utter simplicity and purity. They possessed by descent from Abraham the qualities to provide a material body able to contain the Christ, and—as is mystically shown by the seventy-seven generations of the Lucan genealogy, reaching back beyond the Fall.—they could provide the etheric and astral sheaths into which the young second Adam could descend and mature. Rudolf Steiner rejects the idea of a physical virgin birth, which would make meaningless the paternal genealogy, but he reveals the virginity as a spiritual condition of total absence of sexual desire and passion, the conception being an act in guided unconsciousness, such as is symbolized by some of the Eastern initiatory rites of marriage. More than this hint cannot be given here, but the subject can be followed further in *The Childhood and Youth of Jesus* by Emil Bock.

This Nathan child was as Adam was when man set out to discover his own ego consciousness in earthly experience, but, having never entered on the process of reincarnation, he had in himself only the potentiality of egohood. But there was another quality that he possessed to the full, and that linked him to one of the great religious streams of the past. Six centuries before, Buddha, the great Indian teacher, had discovered and taught that man could escape from what seemed to him the tragedy of reincarnation, not by asceticism and philosophy alone, but by purifying himself on the Eightfold Path of compassion and self knowledge. Thereby Buddha himself escaped from physical reincarnation, but his purified soul continued to exercise its influence from the spirit world. His soul being, filled with the perfection of human compassion, overshadowed and encompassed this paradisal Nathan child from his birth. While the child's lack of earthly ego development made him as yet undeveloped in earthly knowledge and experience, he grew up in the simplicity of spiritual wisdom and was filled with an infinite wealth of love and compassion.

With the Solomon child of the Bethlehem parents the situation was quite different. He was to be the channel through which the descending Christ should take into Himself the whole experience of humanity through all the ages of reincarnating struggle and suffering. While in the Nathan child there was only the innocent potentiality of egohood, in the Solomon child there was incarnated the most fully developed human ego. This was Zarathustra, the greatest of the mighty spiritual leaders of humanity, who had guided mankind through its long pilgrimage of earthly experience. Five thousand years before this great event, he had been the first to perceive and to reveal the meaning of the earthly struggle between good and evil, and to foretell the coming to earth of the great god of Light, who should deliver man from the powers of Darkness. Unlike Buddha, who had been wholly concerned with the individual's path of deliverance, Zarathustra was the revealer of the cosmic will and purpose within which man was placed. Through his indwelling inspiration in Hermes and Moses he had shaped the great religions of Egypt and of the Hebrews, and through his reincarnation in Persia in the sixth century B.C. as Zarathos or Zoroaster he had inspired the mystic wisdom of the Greek Pythagoras, and had planted in the exiled Hebrew prophets the hope of the coming of the Messiah. He whose supreme spiritual wisdom could have lifted him from the necessity of reincarnation, had returned to earth again and again in the service of humanity. Now he is to be incarnated in a Hebrew body, that his supremely developed ego may prepare the vehicle in which the Divine Ego, the Ahura Mazdao he had visioned five thousand years before, may dwell.

To do him worship and honour came three Persian Magi from the East, who had seen in the skies the star that told his birth. This star was no material heavenly body, but the spiritual manifestation of him who was Zoroaster, the bright and shining Star, who, they knew, would return as King of the Hebrew people, to make possible the long-foreseen advent of the Christ. Then, as St. Matthew relates, there followed the flight into Egypt from the murderous hate of Herod, and, just as the Persian Magi had linked the religion of his early incarnation with his final messianic task, so tradition has it that the little family found shelter in the temple of the Sun Mysteries in Egypt, whose Hermetic wisdom Zarathustra's own spirit had inspired.

Then returning from Egypt, Joseph is warned in a dream not to return to Bethlehem and is directed specifically to Nazareth. There the two families are united and the children grow up together, the Solomon Jesus alert beyond his years with the wisdom of his own great past, and the Nathan Jesus living in dreamy childlike acceptance of his physical surroundings, but shedding over them an aura of paradisal love and gentleness. So they grew, two mighty human beings, the one the resurgence of man's fullest, divinely fashioned potentialities, the other the epitome of man's noblest striving from darkness to light. Thus they provided the two aspects of humanity, both of which were essential to the redeeming, restoring work of the incarnating Christ, but as yet they were not united in one personality.

In the gospel narratives there is almost complete silence between the nativity stories and the baptism of Jesus in his full manhood. It is Luke who lifts the veil for one moment, in the story of the visit to the Temple of Jerusalem; the lost child and the frantic search, the discovery of an unexpected wisdom that bewildered both doctors and parents. This unfinished sketch is all that is given openly of the great esoteric mystery of the merging into one human personality of the separately evolved vehicles of Incarnation.

The two Jesus boys had arrived at the threshold of adolescence, when their own astral body was emerging into consciousness from the shelter of its maternal astral sheath. To the Nathan child that could only mean an uncomprehending experience of an outer world, to which it carried no clue in its past or in its spirit—derived love. Here Zarathustra makes the first of two great final sacrifices. He leaves his own physical and etheric bodies and, with his awakening astrality, enters into the being of the Nathan Jesus. This change is indicated in the discovery in the Temple of the child, lost and , when found, hardly recoginzable.

These facts Steiner could only discover from the Akashic Record, for of such profound spiritual events little was ever openly recorded. But hints of a knowledge appear from time to time in art.

In the picture "Christ among the Doctors" by Borgognoni in the fifteenth century the mystery is almost revealed. The whole interest in the picture is centred, not on the amazing wisdom of the Nathan boy's questions and answers, or the consequent admiration of the doctors or the surprise of his mother, but on three figures, the mother and the two Jesus boys. In the centre, raised on a dais, sits the Nathan Jesus, while Mary stands in the left foreground, her face bent in wistful compassion toward the wraithlike figure of the Solomon Jesus at her side. It is as if all three were aware of the wondrous event that had taken place, as though the sight of the transformed Nathan Jesus had revealed it. He sits in tranquil self-possession, his face lit with the light of wisdom, and he looks with wistful comprehension toward the fading figure of the other boy, whose face is turned from him. On the face of the Solomon Jesus there is a hauntingly sad look. It is as if his heart had been wrung by the long search for his gentle friend, so little fitted to deal with strange surroundings. But when he finds him sagely disputing, his face lit with wisdom, he turns away from him, knowing that it is for himself that he must grieve, forsaken by the mighty spirit that had expressed itself in him. The doctors sitting around are no longer interested in the wonder child, but look in bewilderment at the sad resignation of the other boy.

They all return to Nazareth and shortly the forsaken sheaths of the Solomon boy pass into the spirit world, and so too does the Nazareth Mary. The old Bethlehem Joseph has already died, and the Bethlehem Mary and the Nathan Jesus are taken into the home of the Nazareth Joseph. Of all this and the next eighteen years the Gospel narrative is silent, but once again from the Akashic record Rudolf Steiner fills in the picture. He describes the patience and reverence that are needed to decipher this Record, but he does it with a restraint and understanding that not only makes his *Fifth Gospel* a worthy accompaniment of the Bible narrative, but throw great illumination upon the continually developing process of the Incarnation.

As he grows, the Nathan Jesus, who in the emergence of his astral body from its maternal sheath had become yet more deeply united with the overshadowing spirit of Buddha, is led and instructed in the awakening of his soul experience of the outer world by the mighty wisdom of the indwelling Zarathustra.

At length he reaches his full ego consciousness as Jesus of Nazareth, never having been conscious—as none of us are conscious—of the higher ego of Zarathustra informing and directing him. Steiner describes how in this matured ego consciousness Jesus passes through the land, absorbing into his soul the tragedy of human sin and suffering, the utter defeat by the evil powers of the spiritual forces of humanity in general, and the utter insufficiency of the spiritual resources of Judaism and even of the Essenes. The Buddha love and compassion, leading to withdrawal from earthly life becomes the Jesus love and compassion, poured forth in sacrificial service of the Earthly destiny of mankind. We have before us the "Son of Man", "the man of sorrows and acquainted with grief."

As Jesus arrives at his full manhood we reach the final sacrifice of Zarathustra. Never has he withdrawn from the call of the vision of Ahura Mazdao five thousand years before. Having sacrificed his physical and etheric bodies that in his astral development he might complete the human perfection that is to be the vehicle of the Christ, now he will withdraw *himself*, his eternal spirit being, from the being of Jesus of Nazareth, fitted at last to be the vehicle of the descending Christ, that the Christ being may dwell in him as his Holier Ego, the Christ whose power and wisdom had, from without, directed and empowered every stage of this preparation.

In Jesus's thirtieth year Zarathustra withdraws, and Jesus feels in his own earthly ego the loss of that power and direction by which he had, unconsciously, been sustained. He moves as in a dream, but by divine guidance, to where John the Baptist is baptizing. He is baptized and "as he comes up out of the water" he receives the baptismal initiation. "He sees the heavens opened and the Holy Spirit in the form of a dove, descending upon him." The Son of God unites Himself with the Son of Man. "A body hast Thou prepared for me. Then said I, Lo! I come to do Thy will."

As the result of the baptismal initiation, Jesus, as Son of Man, is now conscious of Christ as his true ego, as he had never before been conscious of Zarathustra. Christ, as Son of God, is working actively in a perfect human being, who is absolutely conscious of Him and united to Him in complete dedication to His will.

The three years of the Ministry are the continuing work of Christ in entering, as the Divine Word, into complete participation in the divine-human elements in Jesus's personality, astral, etheric and physical, that He might fill them with a divine power that should be available to all men and women. His penetration into the astral is marked in the Gospel by the Temptation, that into the etheric by the Transfiguration, and finally that into the physical by the Cross, whereby "He tasted death for every man." Nor was it until that final cry of triumph rose from the darkness, "It is finished!" that the Incarnation of the Divine Christ into human nature was finally complete.

# ADDENDUM

Dr. Shepherd in a letter written in 1959 points out that in the Dead Sea Scrolls two Messiahs are spoken of "In Jesus, the various functions of both Messiahs have been combined". These Scrolls were discovered long after Rudolf Steiner's death.

# PART THREE

## Carrying Life's Burdens

# 1 THE BURDEN-SHARER[18]

Most of us have got burdens to carry in these difficult days, and some of us very heavy ones. Christ spoke of life's burdens in one of his best-known sayings: *"Come unto me all ye that labour and are heavy-laden, and I will give you rest."* Now to most people **"rest"** means that they will *get rid of* their burdens—and sometimes they grumble that, in spite of their religion, their burdens are still there. But Christ never promised to rid us of all our burdens. What he promised was a *secret of how to deal with them.*

As a matter of fact, that saying of Christ should never be quoted alone—as it generally is—but with the verses that follow it. *"Take my yoke upon you and learn of me; for I am meek and lowly in heart. And ye shall find rest unto your souls. For my yoke is easy and my burden is light."* Nothing here about getting rid of our burdens. See how it begins. **"Take my yoke upon you."** The yoke of course is what a man or an animal wears on his shoulders in order to carry a burden. The first thing then is, **"Put on the yoke. Be ready to carry any burden."**

**"Take my yoke upon you and *learn of me.*"** In other words, **"Yoke yourself alongside of me and we will carry the burden together and I will show you how to do it."** Christ's hearers knew what he meant. They knew that an inexperienced bullock was often double-yoked with an experienced one, in order to learn his task. So Christ does not promise to take away all our burdens, nor to carry them for us. He does not offer to be a burden-bearer, but a *burden-sharer.* And he does not share them merely to take the weight off our shoulders, *but to teach us the secret of carrying them.* No one ever knew more about carrying burdens than Christ did. No one ever carried heavier burdens. No one ever carried them so effectively and so serenely.

There was a secret in it. That is what he wants us to learn. He puts it in eight words. *"For I am meek and lowly in heart."* "Surprising words!" you may well say. "I should have thought that to carry burdens happily you want to be tough and cheerful. But meek and lowly! Does that mean that one is always ready to be put upon; afraid to stand up to anyone? Surely it can't mean that.(?)" Quite right: it doesn't. In fact,

---

18   6 B.B.C. broadcasts October 1952.

meekness is more of an attitude to yourself and to life than to other people. It means—not to have yourself always in the middle of the picture; not to expect to get off better than other people; not to think, "That ought never to have happened to *me*," or "I ought not to have to carry that burden, when others don't have to." And **"lowly"** means—not to think any burden is beneath your dignity. So to be **"meek and lowly"** means *to be able to forget yourself altogether and just take up the burden.* Now that needs "toughness," a much finer sort of toughness than most people mean when they say someone is "tough." If you try to get that meekness and lowliness you will find out what strength of character it demands. It is the toughness of tempered steel that can meet any stress. **"The meek,"** said Christ, **"shall inherit the earth!"**

And that complete selflessness carries *a serene calmness* that is deeper than cheerfulness. Christ calls it **"my peace"** and he offers it to us. **"Ye shall find rest unto your souls."** These words take us to the heart of Christ's secret. It is this. It is not the weakness of our bodies, but the fretfulness of our souls, that makes our burden so unbearable. **"My yoke is easy and my burden is light."** If you have rest in your soul, no burdens are too heavy.

"Grant to us, Lord Christ, the inward serenity that comes from walking yoked with thee; that so, we may bear life's ills and carry life's burdens with thy peace in our hearts."

# 2 THE BURDEN OF SUFFERING

One of the most obvious facts in the world to-day is the vast extent of human suffering, both in body and mind, from illness and from the cruelty of man to man, and from the consequent sorrows of the human heart. Our age is sensitive to suffering; many find in suffering the great stumbling block to their faith. They feel it should not be there at all. I am not thinking about that now, nor about the healing of suffering—important as they both are. I am just thinking of the fact that most of us, sometime or other, have to carry that burden of suffering. What does Christ teach us about carrying it?

The first point you remember is that we must be **"meek,"** that is, *not self-centred.* Now most of us tend to be self-centred in suffering. For instance, we all read about suffering in the papers every day, and we see it all around us. We sympathise, but we accept it as a universal fact of human life. But when it comes to us, we tend to feel *wronged* and *indignant* and *rebellious*. We feel, "That should not have happened to me." Of course its irrational, but nothing makes suffering or sorrow more *unendurable* than when that feeling is there. *It can destroy the whole personality.*

What did Christ say about it? You remember how his disciples felt that the suffering of the Cross surely could not come to him. **"That shall never happen unto *thee*,"** they said. And when it did happen, it knocked them to pieces. But after his resurrection Jesus said to them, **"It is just what you ought to have *expected* the Christ to do, to *achieve his task by the path of suffering*."** What he meant was that the Christ—and any one who tries to follow him—*can only deal with the sin of the world if he is willing to share the suffering sin has brought and still brings into the world.* It is a big thought, but a true thought, that any one who can accept their suffering as part of the world's burden they are asked to carry, *is sharing in the redemptive work of Christ*. This takes a lot of doing! I wouldn't dare offer it to you merely as my advice. But we are thinking of how Christ carried these burdens.

I once knew a delicate, cultured woman who suddenly lost her father and her devoted husband, who had been her strength and stay, and then for three years, watched her only son, a magnificent athlete, die slowly of tuberculosis. It is forty years ago, but I still see her when it was all over—her face marked with sorrow, but her smile serene and her eyes lit, as one who, walking through the fire, had found the Son of God walking beside her, and so had walked unscathed.

There is another egotism in suffering. It is not so devastating, but it is very common. It is *self-pity*, the feeling that, because we suffer, we have a *right to be "looked after,"* a constant and plaintive expectation of sympathy and service from others. There was not a trace of this in Christ. The keynote of his life was, "I came, not that others should help and serve me, but that I should serve and help others." Never had a man more sympathy with human suffering, never did any man spend his life more completely in the active relief of suffering. At the moment of his most intense suffering of body and spirit on the Cross, he looked down and saw his mother and his beloved friend distraught with bewildered sorrow. Out of the depths of his own sorrow he comforted them; and the way of comfort he showed them was, *to comfort one another*. "Be to him his mother; be to her her son." No one can ever really comfort another except out of a personal experience of suffering that has been transformed from a burden to a blessing by sharing it with Christ.—*Then* "the yoke is easy and the burden is light."

"Teach us, O Lord, to walk with thee the path of suffering as the path of service, and so comfort us in our suffering, that we may be able to comfort others, through the comfort by which we ourselves have been comforted by thee."

# 3 THE BURDEN OF SIN

The burden of sin differs in many respects from life's other burdens. In the first place it is a burden that many people carry unconsciously. They don't feel their sins as a burden at all. In the ancient world—even up to the Middle Ages—man did feel this burden, but in our "psychological" age men are advised "*not to take their sins too seriously.*" So, to talk of "the burden of our sins" is to a great many people quite meaningless.

Of course they stumble and fall very often—and sometimes they fall badly—but they never suspect that it is the burden of past sin on their back, that makes their feet unsure. In fact, they feel that the past is over and done with. It can't be helped and it can't matter now. All that matters is the present moment. Sometimes, as they get to middle age, or older, they begin to be conscious of a burden of some sort, when they see that they still stumble and fall in the same way. But they feel, either sadly or cynically, that it is *too late* to do anything about it and that they must just put up with being a moral failure.

Another special fact about the burden of sin is, that we *only become conscious of it when we begin to want to get rid of it,* and that the more we desire this the heavier the burden proves. Just as Christian in *Pilgrims' Progress* felt his burden of sin grow heavier all the way—*until he reached the Cross of Christ.*

Now it is only when we look steadfastly at the Cross of Christ that we realise the burden of our sin. For *there it is,* with all the sins of the world added to it, resting upon the innocent Son of God, who chose to carry it before men's eyes, that they might realise it and so, by his help, get rid of it. What majesty in the meekness that bowed itself to that burden! What love in that lowliness!

As we contemplate it, we begin to realise that that in man—that in ourselves—which made necessary this supreme sacrifice of Divine Innocence, cannot be something which "we need not take too seriously."

On the other hand, if the consciousness of the burden of our sin awakes in us and grows until it seems unbearable, we can be sure that he would not have carried that burden on the Cross, unless he had known that thereby he could lift it from us.

Indeed, in this very invitation to us to come to him, of which we are thinking this week, Christ is *above all* offering to free us from the burden of sin. There are two ways in which that burden weighs us down—when once we become aware of it—firstly by the sense of guilt and shame and separation from God; and secondly, by the repeated realisation of our own helplessness against temptation. In both these directions Christ lifts the burden of sin from our back. For the fact that he, the Son of God, offers to walk yoked with us shows that he does not despair of us. That lifts from us the burden of shame. And if we do yoke ourselves with him and learn of him, we shall at last get the power to overcome temptation. That lifts the burden of despair and defeat.—It doesn't matter how overwhelming our burden of sin seems. It doesn't matter if we have carried it so long that it has almost become part of us. If we listen to this call of Christ, we *can* get rid of it.

What the sense of release from this burden can be, only those who have experienced it know. St. Paul puts it thus. **"If God accepts us, what does it matter who condemns us? If God is on our side, what power can defeat us? From the love of Christ that has freed us from the burden of our sin nothing can ever again separate us. In everything—temptation, suffering, persecution, anxiety, life's daily duties—we are more than conquerors, through him that loved us."**

# 4 THE BURDEN OF RESENTMENT

Of all the burdens men carry none is more *galling* than the burden of resentment. I am speaking, of course, of personal resentment, not of indignation against wrong done to others. Personal resentment is a burden that one cannot get used to; we feel it more the longer we carry it, until it becomes *almost unbearable.* How does Christ teach us to deal with this burden?

Well, it was a burden he never carried himself. He had laid upon him a great burden of wrong and ingratitude, but he never added to it the burden of resentment. For he was "meek," that is, not self-centred. When Christ was wronged, he did not think about himself. He only thought how those who were wronging him were implicating themselves in the terrible tangle of evil and ill-will in which mankind is bound. So, as the nails drove through his hands, he cried, **"Forgive them, for they know not what they do."** They *didn't* know. Men don't realise the inevitable consequences of wrong-doing, with its ever-widening wake of ill-will, and with its moral consequences that are even more inevitable and devastating *after death* than before. There was *only one way* to cut through this tangle of wrong and ill-will and moral consequence and that was *the way of forgiveness.* Christ redeemed the sin of the world by forgiving it.

If you ask Christ how to deal with this burden of resentment which is eating into your heart, he says, "This is one of life's burdens you can get rid of yourself. Stop being resentful and forgive." And if you exclaim, "But he—or she—has spoilt my whole life!" he replies, "By far the greatest harm he has done to you is to make you resentful. It is poisoning your soul. *Why do you let him do that to you?* Drop your resentment and then the only burden on your shoulders will be the suffering he has caused you. If you carry that bravely, knowing it to be undeserved, it will not gall you. And that burden *I can share with you.* "

Now there are hundreds of people who honestly think themselves to be Christians, to whom the command to forgive injuries appears quite impossible. It seems to them a sign of weakness. Of course it isn't. It's the sign of divinity. **"Forgive your enemies,"** Christ said, **"that ye may be sons of your Father in heaven. For He is always forgiving."** *Forgiveness is the distinctively divine deed.*

Moreover, a refusal to forgive carries a very big risk. In one way your resentment is correct. The wrongdoer, if he does not repent and seek forgiveness, will pay, at any rate after death, the full moral consequences of his deed. But, if you keep up your resentment, *so will you!* Perhaps for some share in that very wrong you hold against him. But also for *your own* wrong deeds! For if you hold another to the consequences of his misdeeds, you obviously cannot escape the same terms being applied to you. **"With what judgement ye judge, ye shall be judged,"** said Christ. Now you see what he meant. That is why those who won't forgive, *cannot* enter into the experience of being forgiven themselves. Christ warned us about this more than once.

But to forgive is not only to safeguard your own forgiveness. It is *to share in the redeeming work of Christ.* For, when you forgive, you stop the flow of a stream of ill-will that otherwise will flow on into eternity. But most wonderful of all—*human forgiveness is a mirror in which many a wrongdoer has seen in reflection, for the first time, the Cross of Christ.*

The Burden of Resentment, then, is one that you need not carry, and the way of release is—to forgive! Once you really forgive and let that burden of resentment go, you will feel that a crushing weight has slipped off your shoulders and that your own soul is lifted clear, above all power of human evil to touch it, and that you are really walking side by side with Christ.

**"Reveal to us, O Christ, the nobility and grandeur of thy divine forgiveness which nothing can deter, that it may purge from our hearts the bitterness and ignominy of resentment."**

# 5 THE BURDEN OF ANXIETY

Worry is the most common burden of humanity. Christ spoke about it many times. It was his great compassion for humanity that marked how men and women were bowed down under this burden of anxiety. For the most part, in those days, it was the burden of poverty, the uncertainty of getting the necessities of life.—But it was not only compassion for their material needs that moved him, but for *the spiritual desolation* that resulted from their anxiety. "Do not *worry* yourself about *to-morrow,*" he said. That is the *exact* meaning of his words. He did not mean that they should not exercise proper foresight, but that they should not be so absorbed in to-morrow's hopes and fears that they gave no heed to the present and even hardly noticed the good news he was bringing to them. The danger was that in their anxiety about material things, food and clothes, they lost sight of the higher values, the real *needs* of the *life* they were seeking to *feed,* or the *true glory* of the *body* they strove to *clothe.*

To-day we live in the age of the Welfare State, in which we are secured against the stark necessities of poverty, sickness or unemployment. But we still have worries; anxiety about getting a house, about making the rations do[19], about rising prices or the possibility of another war. The danger of losing the higher values is still with us. Indeed, if we come to think that material well-being is the *one* ideal of the Welfare state, the old anxieties can easily be turned into longings for still more *material* benefits, an ever-higher standard of living, television sets, motor cars; forgetting *the sort of national character,* which alone makes a Welfare State a blessing and not a snare to a nation.

---

[19] Rationing was still in force in 1952.

Another danger arising out of the anxiety is the fear that it breeds. Fear is the enemy of true spiritual development. Christ was always telling his disciples not to be afraid. **"Don't live in to-morrow's fears,"** he said. **"If they ever do materialise, they belong to to-morrow and only in that to-morrow can they be dealt with. At this moment they are a useless distraction from grasping to-day's opportunities."**

I once knew a little old woman who was a fairy godmother in the street of poor houses in which she lived. Everyone came to her for comfort and advice. She was always busy and always happy.—She had been born without fingers on her hands. She told me once, "My mother used to cry for hours as to what would become of me, because of my hands. But I *knew God* would look after me, and I haven't found there was anything I couldn't do—except button up my gloves!" She had never let fear for the future blind her to the possibilities of the present. And her neighbours came to her with their worries, because they knew *she* had *conquered worry*.

But the greatest evil of anxiety is that it is a complete faithlessness in the continual concern of God with the life of each one of us, which is what "Providence" means. Nothing is more positive in the teaching of Jesus than what he says about this. The whole physical life of this world, he taught, is upheld by divine care and spiritual activity. Even with a sparrow, with the very hairs of your head, with each one of you individually. God knows your need of material things. Strive each day to fulfil His purpose for you—and leave the rest to Him, and all will be well. Thousands have proved this to be true.

But it wasn't only teaching that Christ gave, but example. He could see in his own life the dark shadows of the future, his cross and passion, the uncomprehending collapse of his disciples, the inevitable destruction of his beloved nation, the faithlessness of unborn generations. But *nothing* could disturb *his serene concentration* on the immediate task His Father had given him. **"My meat is to do the will of Him that sent me and to finish his work."**

With Christ as our yoke-fellow in life, we shall make so many discoveries of *God's concern for us* and be so absorbed in our task for him, that we can never be anxious about the future, because we know that there we shall still have Christ walking with us.

**"Deliver us, O Lord, we beseech thee, from the unbeliefs and fears of our faithless hearts, and so fill us with a sense of thy power and willingness to supply all our needs, that nothing may seem too**

great or too hard to undertake at thy call, and that we may continually rejoice in thy sufficiency."

# 6 THE BURDEN OF DULLNESS

I can imagine some who may have been listening to these talks saying, "I haven't got in my life *any* of these burdens you have been speaking of. Perhaps it would be better if I had. I might at least have got some 'kick' out of it. My life is just *plumb dull*, the same job all the year and every year. I meet the same folk, I do the same things. I don't see how God can have any special use for a life as dull as mine."

Well of course, the fact is that you are carrying a burden—without knowing it. It is not one of those galling, wearing burdens that I've been speaking about, but it is a burden all the same, the burden of dullness!

If ever anyone needed to yoke himself alongside Christ, you do. For Christ turned a life that most people would have thought dull, into a continual adventure for God. His own townsfolk felt that his life was so ordinary that they couldn't believe he could be making a stir anywhere. "We know him. He's the village carpenter, and his mother and sisters live down the street. A man with a background like that can't work wonders."

But wherever Jesus went, he made a unique occasion out of the most ordinary circumstances. Resting on a hot morning on a well-side, and passing the time of day with an ignorant woman, he lit a flame in her heart that brought her whole village to the truth. Catching sight another day of an inquisitive face, peering at him through the leaves of a tree, he invited himself to dinner and changed a hard-boiled swindler into a generous-hearted child of God. Walking through a cornfield with it scarlet poppies, he saw and revealed the providence of God, and the mystery of His ways with the souls of men.

In what other men would have called commonplace situations he found adventures for God—*because he was always on the look-out for them. That was his secret.* That attitude can turn the dullest circumstance into an adventure. I remember a young builder telling me once, "I never knew how exciting life could be, until I began to look for opportunities of doing things for others."

So it can be in what you call your "plum dull" life. Your burden of dullness you can drop whenever you like. In fact, if you yoke your life with Christ, it will disappear of itself, and you will find adventure for

God everywhere—in your own family, among those you work with or happen to meet. The only condition is—*that you expect to find it.*

      \*      \*      \*

Thus we have seen how in this wonderful invitation, Christ offers to show mankind how to deal with life's burdens. Some he helps us to carry, others he teaches us to throw away as unnecessary, others he dispels. The burden of sin he takes upon himself.

But it is not only deliverance from the crushing weight of our own burdens that comes to us from taking Christ as our companion and keeping in step with him. *We also learn to be—like him—a burden-sharer.* Every man must carry his own burden, St. Paul reminds us; that is, he must put his shoulder to it. He must not rebel or refuse. But he must *also* be ready to put his shoulder to *his brother's* burden and share it with him. For some are overburden, some have lost heart and courage, and most have never heard Christ's invitation. So, as we find rest of soul from our own burdens, let us seek to bear one another's burdens—*"and so fulfil the law of Christ"*—*the Burden-sharer of all mankind.*

Let us, in conclusion listen once again to his words, which he speaks to each one of us.

**"Come unto me all ye that labour and are heavy-laden, and I will give you rest. Take my yoke upon you and learn of me; for I am meek and lowly in heart. And ye shall find rest unto your souls. For my yoke is easy and my burden is light."**

# APPENDIX

# THE SERMON 24<sup>th</sup> June 1952.[20]

Philippians 1.7.

> **"I have you in my heart, inasmuch as, both in my bonds and in the defence and confirmation of the gospel, ye all are partakers with me of grace."**

In many ways this consecration service in which we are engaged has a unique character. It is the first occasion on which a bishop has been consecrated in Worcester Cathedral in the nine hundred years of its history. Except by special permission, a bishop, consecrated in the province of Canterbury, has to be consecrated in the Archiepiscopal seat of the Archbishop at Canterbury or in London. The kindness of the Archbishop in coming to Worcester has made possible what can seldom take place, namely that our brother is being consecrated bishop in the midst of the people of the diocese in which he has served all his ministry and out of which he has been called to his new task in Northern Nigeria.

Through his work as Diocesan Youth Organiser John Mort is known to almost all his brother clergy and in almost every parish in the diocese, while from the two parishes of Dudley and St. John, Worcester, in which he has worked as assistant curate and vicar, a very large number are present at this service. It is, moreover, surely almost unique that he is being presented to the Archbishop by the Bishop and the Assistant Bishop of his own diocese, both of whom have given a lifetime of service in missionary work, Bishop Lasbrey having been for many years Bishop of the neighbouring diocese to that from which the new diocese of Northern Nigeria is being taken.

But above and beyond its special setting and circumstances, it is the service of consecration itself, which very many of us will be witnessing

---

[20] The sermon preached by the Venerable A. P. Shepherd D.D., Canon of Worcester, at the CONSECRATION at Worcester Cathedral by the Most Reverend the Lord Archbishop of Canterbury of the Rev. John Ernest Llewelyn Mort M. A. as Bishop of Northern Nigeria on the Feast of St. John the Baptist, 24th June 1952.

for the first time, that should hold our reverent attention, and appeal to our deepest religious feelings. The rite of the consecration of a bishop is one of the most solemn and awe-inspiring services in the Christian Church. Our Lord Jesus Christ founded His Church to be His Body, by means of which the Holy Spirit should work manifestly in and through the lives of men and women. By Baptism and Confirmation every Christian becomes in his or her daily life the instrument of the Holy Spirit. Through Ordination men are set apart to be the human channels through which the divine forgiveness and the divine life are imparted. But in the consecration of a bishop a man is set apart, not only to be the overseer and governor of the flock committed to his charge, but also to be the instrument through which alone the other ministries of the Spirit can be bestowed on the laity and the priesthood. The bishop is as it were the most direct and immediate human channel through which the Holy Spirit exercises his life-giving and regenerating work in the world. So weighty and solemn is this office that a bishop can only be consecrated to it by the Archbishop, acting with a number of other bishops,

Furthermore, the service of the consecration of a bishop has a special significance in regard to the whole Church. It is the outward and visible sign of the historical and spiritual continuity of the church. As long ago as the fourth century Augustine declared it to be one of the great proofs of the divine nature and authority of the Church that she had faithfully transmitted the teaching of the Apostles in the New Testament and had kept the episcopal sees in direct succession down to the bishops of his day. We, fifteen hundred years later, are witnessing today that same continuous transmission of the divine grace.

Now no man called by the Holy Spirit to this high office can feel himself to be anything but unworthy. No human gifts and abilities, however great, can make him adequate to the task. He needs and, indeed, is wholly dependent upon the outpouring of supernatural grace, which we must strive to realise in the act of consecration as an actual spiritual happening.

It is not enough, however, that we should uphold our brother with our prayers at this his consecration. He will need our prayers continually— and especially as he begins his new work. Here, in Worcester, he has been working in a Christian environment a thousand years old, in close fellowship with very many brother-priests, in the midst of a warm-hearted parish and supported by many faithful and enthusiastic workers. In Northern Nigeria he will be laying the foundations of a new diocese, the leader of a comparative handful of Christian priests and workers separated for the most part from each other by great distances and in the midst of a heathen population. In the exercise, in such surroundings, of his responsible office of bishop he will need continually the assurance that he is supported by our remembrance and our prayers.

It was in his letter to his beloved Church at Philippi, which was the base of his missionary work in Europe, as Antioch had been in Asia, and which had kept continually alive by its prayers and gifts the love which had sprung up between him and them during his ministry there, that St. Paul wrote, from his trials and sufferings in Rome, those wonderful words which I have taken as my text. I will repeat them again in a slightly amended form that will make their meaning clearer to us today.

> **"I have you in my heart, inasmuch as, both in the obstacles which confront me and in my task of defending and establishing the gospel, you are all partakers with me of the grace which I have received."**

I am sure that there will be many occasions in which our brother will be facing, almost alone, new and responsible decisions, when it will make all the difference to him if he can feel that he has his friends in his heart, as sharing with him by their prayers in his missionary task and in the grace of God which he will have received for it.

Just as this wonderful rite of episcopal consecration both creates and symbolises the unity of the Church which overleaps the passage of time, so the true fellowship of prayer and love bridges the distance of space that separates Christian from Christian and annihilates any sense of loneliness, in the consciousness that we have each other in our hearts as sharers in one another's tasks and partakers of the same divine grace. This is, here and now, the experience of the communion of saints.

My dear brother, since you came to me as a deacon twelve years ago to the parish church of Dudley, I have watched and will always watch with affection and interest the development of your ministerial work and I count it a great privilege to have been asked to preach the sermon at this service. As you are upheld today, in this solemn moment of your consecration, by the presence and prayers of this great congregation, so may the remembrance and continuance of our spiritual fellowship ever strengthen you in the discharge of your episcopal ministry. We shall have you in our hearts. May God have you in His keeping.

# Indx

## — A —

## — B —

## — C —

## — D —

## — E —

## — F —

## — G —

## — H —

## — I —

## — J —

## — K —